VISION OF AN
ENLIGHTENED WORLD

Anup Rej

VISION OF AN ENLIGHTENED WORLD

A Cosmic Perspective

www.booksofexistence.no

After the book was conceived in Norway it was partly written while the author visited Chiang Mai, Phyao and Chiang Rai in Northern Thailand in December 2012 and partly in Dhaka, where the author`s wife had served as the Ambassador of Norway to Bangladesh (2010-2013).

A CALL FOR CHANGE IN THE PRESENT WORLD-ORDER

"Replace the present world-order, which has been shaped mostly by the actions, will and freedom nurtured by the instincts of man, by an enlightened world, which may project the higher realm of consciousness of the human mind. Instead of building a society, which inspires man to grab, compete, dominate and exploit the weaker fellow beings by using the existing economic and military disparities in the world, let us aspire for creating an enlightened-society where human beings may find meaning of life in sharing one`s knowledge, innovation and creative abilities for the benefit of the mankind as a whole. By empowering, guiding and teaching the fellow human beings about the "higher-nature" residing in ourselves let us pave the path of fulfilling the meaning of human existence as the bearer of a great cosmic mind."

List of contents

Preface

Since 1990s the world has undergone a fast transformation helped by the demise of the communists in the Soviet Union and rising monopoly of power of the capitalist ideology which emphasizes on free market competition. The biggest change has been brought by economic globalization where capitalism has taken the driving seat in steering the economic growth of the world. Even countries like China and India have succumbed to its force. Free flow of capital and investment, without state control, has been the main motor behind this globalization drive. It has been followed by development in the communication technology, which has tied remote corners of the world together. The resource management and manpower utilization have cut across the traditional economic patterns and outsourcing measures have given more advanced economies of the world the opportunities to make use of the man-power in the low-income countries. It has become a new mode of the global economic activities. Together with it the access to information about the labour-cost, raw material and possibility of profits from investments in different political environment have added the utility of the mobile and digital technology in accelerating the economic globalization. Moreover, the modern communication these days does not leave any area of life outside the zone of infiltration of the market. The ideology which professes profits in all endeavours of life, has ensnared all cultures. In resonance with the free market economy, the ideas of the human rights and democracy have also gained gradual ascendance. In the capitalist world the freedom of the individuals to freely decide over one`s political and civil behaviour play pivotal role. In these countries human rights is seen as individual`s rights to freely choose and associate with ideas in order to participate in choosing the

1

way the society may be governed without being coerced by force, or intimidation. In this social philosophy, democracy and human rights are considered as the basic pillars of development and progress of a society. On the other hand the countries, which had a socialist past together with some poorer nations, who need developmental help from richer countries, emphasize on the human rights as collective economic development and rights of the people as a whole, instead.

The drive for more democracies and freedom resulting in economic development and growth across the globe, have given rise to a world-wide expansion of the consumer culture and brought forth a breakdown of the traditional values in many societies. The consumer culture has infiltrated and seduced all social classes everywhere. However, the middle class has become the major fan bearer of such economic growth in those countries, who until the Second World War, remained under the colonial rules. The increase in consumer culture, which in its turn is based on higher consumption and an unbalanced utilization of resources of nature, has brought impacts on the global environment. It is believed that the economic development, which needs higher fuel consumption and unbalanced utilization of the natural resources, has already turned into a threat to the world. The extreme weather patterns seen in recent years seem to confirm the consequences of human economic activities afflicting the climate. While most nations of the world, under the military dominations of a few countries enjoying advance economies, are being seduced to follow the capitalistic path, there are not many possibilities to work outside the present social-political order by any other means than by following the democratic prescription professed by the West. To counteract this development by any military or economic means seems remote. Some adversaries of the western powers have adopted the path of terror in trying to bring changes - like the religious groups within Islam who wish to fight the power of the US and its allies in the West. In the pursuit of containing terrorism, the western powers make use of the advance technologies to spy on whoever they wish to control. By this way they often foil attempts of terrorist acts. This world-wide surveillance also spreads its tentacles in other areas involving economic and military interests, so that no nation or group may challenge the hegemony of the present world-order within a foreseeable future.

Historical backdrop

The present world-order is a direct consequence of the colonial history and the progress of industrialization which occurred during that time. Today`s world may be characterized by the following disparities

> •The economic and political power are dominated by the old colonial powers of Europe in alliance with the US and Canada, where the migrants from Britain and France formed their independent states.
> •The banking and financial systems of the world are fully under the control of the major powers of Europe and the US.
> •The old colonial powers of Europe together witth the US maintain a technological and military superiority over the rest of the world.
> •The energy resources, which are backbones of the economic development and modern living standard are under the control of the old colonial powers and the US.
> •The oil and gas resources in the world are being protected by authoritarian local cronies looking after the interests of the Western economy.
> •The former colonies are becoming a market for the global investors in the West while the capitals are getting concentrated in fewer and fewer hands.
> •A technocratic elite is emerging in the older colonies, who carry out the globalization and democratic processes professed by the West, the World Bank and the International Monetary Fund which are under the control of a few powerful players.
> •Vast mass of the population of the world is living under poverty without enjoying the basic rights to food, education and health while democracy and free market consumerism are on the rise.

Old and new actors

The bankers and the industrial entrepreneurs, who came to power with the rise of the colonial trading and in the wake of the industrial civilization in the West, are still the major actors in the world-stage. After the Second World War, the communication equipment and automobiles became parts of the consumer goods. Then came the entertainment industry in the form of television and video equipment. The electronic goods, supporting the music and video industry, flooded the globe with western culture and values. Next came the digital communication age of the internet, which was then followed by the social networking sites like Facebook and Twitter. Everywhere the free market made its way. The private space of daily life turned into a part of the public market place. More one infiltrated into the private space, there increased more opportunities to advertise, manipulate and access information which were useful in controlling and channelling the will of the people towards a consumer oriented society. Thus the present world-order and the power structure behind it took a solid grip. With the rising need for customers in the market oriented democracy, which once rose as a result of the struggle for power by the rising groups of bankers and industrialists against the feudal lords and monarchies enjoying the power and wealth in the colonial time, got newer dimension. More people consumed more the established world-order could boast of growth of freedom of the individuals whose freewill were fully integrated in the market system. With the propagation of entertainments through the new media involving violence, sexual aberrations and promiscuity, drugs, treacheries, espionage and crimes, the producers of the electronic goods became highly successful. With this cultural transformation the traditional values of the society came under the onslaught of the market power.

Apart from the consumer based industries supplying electronic goods to the mass, the industrial giants also invested in the military sector and in the production of oil, gas and mineral resources. Defense against enemies, who may try to thwart the progress and sustainability of the present world-order, was thrown as major arguments for military buildup and need for new technological innovation to conduct warfare. The industry around cyber warfare, which aims to disable the capacity of the enemies to communicate and make the opponents` war machine effectively useless became another big business in the world.

Old and new ideas of governance

In this present economic-political order the idea of democracy has got preponderance. After the demise of the emperors and monarchs the ideas of democracy began with the demand of the rising class to participate in the decision making process of the society. To begin with it was stimulated by the ambitions of the bankers and industrialists who wished to break the monopoly of power of the feudal lords. Demand for democracy and rights of participation of a larger number of the citizens became more vocal with the rising need to dethrone feudalism from power and instead institute the grip of the industrial class in forming the society. With the rise of science and technology, a new educated elite took the opportunities of political openness of the time. They rose to counteract the ambitions of the capitalists in turn. The capitalism was challenged by the socialist ideas, where workers were seen as the bearer of social development. Mainly the middle class intellectuals became the leaders of this socialist ideology. The battle between the socialist and the capitalist saw its end with the demise of the Soviet Union and adoption of capitalistic economic path by the Peoples Republic of China. India emerged as the biggest democracy in the world, where hundreds of millions of illiterates got their rights to vote and choose the party which may govern.

After the failure of socialism, the democracy in a country like India has taken the form of appeasing the mass by various means. From tempting them with ideas related to religious dogmatism and caste and kinship to choosing favourite movie stars and sportsmen as political players have carried the foundation of free choice aided by the entertainment industry. The democracy is fuelling growth of the consumer industry, especially led by the middle class, who are the biggest users of the communication networks which have infiltrated the private space. More consumerism is leading to higher concentration of the wealth and monopoly of the capitalists. More the capitalism is demanding individual freedom more easy it is becoming for the market to invade culture, values and private space of the consumers. Freedom to consume and rise of democracy are going hands in hands. The democracy is becoming the flag bearer of the world-order promoting globalization. The illiterates, who have no understanding of what is going on in the world outside their poverty stricken neighbourhood, and the life shown on the TV screens, are being used as rubber stamps to legalize this process of governance and the development of the society. This form of democracy, which reaps benefits for the consumer industry, and thus drives economic growth, is also sowing some abstruse aspect of change which are not envisioned by the market forces. The illiterates, minorities and dejected in the society are finding platforms of agitation, and thus they are rising to challenge the hegemony of the rich and the powerful through electoral procedures. If the momentum of democracy, as seen in India, can be maintained, the democracy may emerge with a new face where traditional monopoly reserved for the industrial class, in alliance with the financial giants, may one day break down and give rise to a new form of social-order that may empower the weak and the exploited in the society. However, without dismantling the war machineries and the industries around high-tech warfare, it is difficult to envision such a change for the future. Until then the global-order will remain a victim of manipulation and control by the traditional players who have decided the fate of humanity for the last few centuries as the masters of the industrial civilization.

Apart from the potential prospect that the wretched part of humanity may rise one day from the bottom of the social structure, the new major beneficiaries of the present development are the technocrats and the people controlling and affecting the evolution of the communication industry. The digital network services and technologies, which bring people across the globe together in order to exchange ideologies, values and visions of building a new world-order, are becoming the new arbitrators for the future. Once the industrialists, bankers and military establishment become more and more dependent on this class of IT-people living in the cyberspace, the world may one day take a new turn away from the traditional players. This IT-generation may evolve from all economic strata of the society and from everywhere on the globe without any boundary of class, creed and stigma from the colonial era.

Conflicts, contradictions and challenges today

Thus the world is undergoing rapid transformation since the demise of socialism in the Soviet Union and with it the increasing ability of the US to dictate the world affairs at its own terms. However, with the opening up of the Soviet Union to the capitalist economy and gradual integration of the economy of China in the same fold, the world is seeing the development of contradictions which seems to be polarizing the world into two distinct groups: On one side is the old colonial powers allied with the US, and on the other side are the former colonies like India and China allied with Russia. The western powers are joined together in a military alliance of NATO, who maintains a military superiority in the world. The rising Asian economies are striving to build an economic and a political front against the western hegemony by forming a bloc with Russia, Brazil and South Africa which is known as BRICS.

These two worlds are apprehensive of each others` motives of world domination and both sides are moving accordingly on a geo-political tight rope. The western powers use human rights and democracy as their instruments to penetrate and weaken the power of these rising BRICS nations. By offering more consumer culture, and opening up entertainment industry showing mostly violence and crime, and inspiring freedom to disavow traditions and cultures, the western strategists are trying to get the opinions of the population in the economically rising nations on their side. The ideas of democracy and rights of the individuals to execute one`s freedom to act and impart will to protect one`s likings and interests are being used as effective means to counteract the sympathy for the opponents, who often need to use authoritarian means to bring free will of the individuals to submission in order to achieve the common good of the people. By seducing people by the western notions of human rights and the consumer oriented democracy one side is trying to draw people to the economic market ideology where there exists little constraints based on moral judgment. On the other side the BRICS nations reap the sentiments against colonialism and imperialism of the west.

The major geo-political tension arises due to the ascendance of India and China as major economic powers outside the western club (which also includes Japan) and the bleak prospect of the western economies to keep its previous dominance as it has done for several centuries in the past. This economic competition boils down to the access to energy resources like oil and gas. The west has maintained its hegemony over the energy flow by controlling the supply of oil from the Middle East and North Africa. The energy issue has also brought Russia against the West. Russia uses its oil and gas as a bargaining chip against the nations of Europe, who in turn tries to encircle Russia by NATO and create difficulties for Russian economy by using its hegemony over the financial and banking system in the world. While the West charges Russia and China for human rights violations and lack of democracy, the BRICS nations try to create a parallel banking system and financial exchange which will be less dependent on the western reprisal. Amidst this East-West confrontation around the energy resources, the west is trying to secure its supplies from the Middle East and North Africa by putting the rulers of their choice in those nations who would supply them gas and oil. Human rights and democracy are applied and rejected in ways befitting the needs of the situation that may bring forth the desired power change. Military means have been used to bring such changes in recent time. In a reciprocal manner Russia has also used its military muscles to secure its geo-political interests in Ukraine, through which the Russian gas pipelines pass to the European market.

The digital communication revolution is also being utilized in trying to bring desired political adjustments. Recently the political upheaval across the Middle East was orchestrated by making use of social networking, like FaceBook and Twitter. They were advertised by the West as spontaneous uprising of the people against the oppressive regimes, while others saw western plans in using the new communication technology to bring political changes in regions of vital interests for the West. So, propaganda and counter propaganda in the name of democracy, human rights and freedom have become a normal mode of operations in order to bring the political tides on one's favor. The journalism and truthfulness of information through news media have also become questionable due to the partition views split between the East and the West.

Another important competition in the geo-political tug-of-war is to achieve economic growth surpassing the opponents, which in turn hinges on the oil and gas consumption. More fuel burning cause more carbon di oxide pollution of the globe, which is believed to create impacts on altering the climate of Earth. The extreme weathers, observed in recent years, have been attributed to such environmental pollution caused by the increased consumer culture spreading across the globe. The West wants to contain the pollution caused by the productions in China, India and other rising economies, while the others squarely put the blame of the climate change on the West. Instead the poorer nations ask for economic compensation from the West for bringing upon them harsher natural predicaments. Thus environmental issue has become another area of contention. The West wants to carry on its consumption pattern and enjoyment of the standard of life as usual, while devising means that would leave the responsibility of reduction of pollution on the shoulder of the newly rising economies of the East. The military and the financial might of the West is still much superior than the rising Asian powers and it is difficult at the moment to stand against the hegemony of the West, who can easily gather support around its cause among many nations of the world who are still dependent on the Western assistance for development and progress. The only means to harass the West has been the terrorism, which are isolated attacks by small number of people who manage to plant themselves in the society in order to cause harm. Many of these terrorists, in turn, are fostered by intelligence agencies in order to use them in political struggle against the governments who one may wish to replace. Sometimes the terrorism backfires against the powers, who they are supposed to serve. One such issue is the Islamic terrorism who vows to attack the US interests. The US, in turn, has its extensive spying and surveillance network to counteract such threats of terrorism. This surveillance has become all embracing including tapping of telephones, internet browsing and the activities in the social network of most citizens of the globe who make use of these facilities. Freedom of conversation and information exchange has thus become victim in the invisible net of the cyber space which can listen and record all what are being said or exchanged. Freedom is turning into an illusory concept, mostly confined to the right to consume as economic animals in the global market.

Can we envisage any better world?

Given the history which has shaped the world-order of today, and understanding the contradictions and conflicts, which have followed the events of history leading to where we are, one may ask are there any better ways to build the social-political order of the globe than what has descended on mankind from the past? What could be such a world-order which may guide mankind away from the greed for power and hunger for personal freedom and wealth as in the capitalistic system professes, or the intimidation of the individual freedom and self-development under the dictatorship of the proletariats as the socialist system dictates? In the time of history where monarch and despots still ruled, slavery and exploitation were widespread, the religious teachings were the main source of knowledge for the mass who acted under the fear of Heaven and its retribution, the philosophical ideas of freedom, equality and justice sowed the seeds of change. Those who planted these ideas in the political life became the bearer of enlightenment to the world.

Since then the world has gone through the abolition of slavery, eradication of the powers of the feudal lords and introduction of the power of the people to participate in the democratic decision making process in the society. After the end of the Second World War, when the United Nations was formed, it made the ideas coined by the enlightenment philosophers, during the American Independence and the French Revolution, the foundation for building a global society by adopting a Universal Declaration of Human Rights. They were seen as inalienable legal rights for all which should be part of the national and international legislatures. The respect for human rights was seen as the foundation of freedom, justice and peace in the world.

To make a Declaration is one thing and to realize it is of course another matter. The specific rights which should be respected for all human beings were spelled out in two Human Rights Covenants: One on Civil and Political Rights and the other on Economic, Social and Cultural Rights. These covenants came into effect only 38 years ago (in 1976). The covenant on civil and political rights of the individuals include the rights to life, freedom of religion, freedom of speech and freedom of assembly among others, while the economic, social and cultural rights include labour rights, rights to health, education and adequate standard of living. Most countries of the world have by now ratified and agreed to respect these rights. However, the most powerful country, the US, who sees itself as the flag bearer of human rights in the world, has not yet (until 2014) ratified the Covenant on Economic, Social and Cultural Rights of people.

Although majority of countries have ratified these instruments of human rights which legally bind the individual states to respect and safeguard the rights of its people, the world is still in a dire state, where violations of human rights are endemic. The situation in the world is far from fulfilling the enlightened philosophy of 250 years ago. Instead human rights and democracy are mainly used for achieving political gains by stirring protests among groups, who are powerful enough to oust the authoritarian government in power. In the geopolitical battle, which rages these days, the countries of the West are playing their neocolonial game by fanning discontent around the rights of civic and political liberty of the individuals while being aided by the modern social networking facilities.

Given the state of democracy and human rights in the world today, understanding the geopolitical tug-of-war between the West and the rising nations of the East, observing the methods of stirring population and bringing change of government in order to secure the oil and gas supply, noting the rising power of the monopoly capitalism in the global market, being mindful of the prospect of terrorist attacks which may threaten the peace and stability in the world, accepting the widespread surveillance of the population of Earth using high-tech capabilities of the technologically advanced nations, remembering that freedom and liberty has become synonymous with the consumer freedom of a small population of Earth squandering resources of the globe at will, remaining apprehensive of the catastrophic consequences which may follow due to the climate change caused by human behaviour, feeling aghast about the moral decadence brought forth by the present economic and technological development t one wonders what kind of enlightenment may bring this civilization out of this dark tunnel.

In this age when we are becoming prisoners of power of money and technology, and turning into slaves of systems which keep watch on even our private life, we may need ideas of new enlightenment philosophers, who may show us the path of freedom and liberty conducive to evolution towards a higher state of civilization. This book is an attempt to sow seeds of such an Enlightened Age.

INTRODUCTION

War in Afghanistan; the terror of the jihadists in Pakistan; hostage-taking in the oil fields of Algeria; the murder of the US Ambassador in Libya; mass protests in Tahrir Square in Cairo, Egypt; civil war in Syria; the nuclear ambitions of Iran and their challenges to the West; these are some of the stories which have dominated newspapers and the television prime-time news recently, and all around the world. Similarly, news of the cyclones, floods, and other large-scale natural catastrophes believed to have been caused by the changes in the global climate, are taking on greater and greater economic and political significance.

Excessive burning of oil for industrial and transport needs, which is increasing with the growth of the consumer economy, is resulting in the environmental pollution helping to warm up the globe. The hotter globe is causing disruption to normal climate patterns. Scientists predict that with global warming, the sea level may rise due to the melting of ice at the poles, which will threaten to inundate the coastal areas of many countries.

While excessive consumption of energy is causing these climate hazards, at the same time, the demands are rising for more energy, needed to sustain the economic growth of the globalized economy. Together with monetary speculations and the "casino" culture of bankers and speculators, it is bringing greater and greater challenges to the stability of the world economy. Recently, the economic crisis in the Euro zone and the global financial crisis of 2007-2008 are taking a toll on world affairs. They have caused a severe unemployment problem, especially for youths, and have caused political turmoil in many places.

At the same time, technology development is progressing and social networks are spreading fast amongst youths. They are becoming instruments for organizing protests and agitations, and are thus turning the political scene in different directions. In some places, religious fundamentalisms are on a march. The world is struggling to contain the development led by religious groups, who want to bring changes by adopting methods of terror.

Amidst this turmoil, consumer culture is spreading all over the world. Consumerism is causing traditional values to give way to the market-oriented values of the modern lifestyle. With the illusion of attaining a happier life, the middle class, in particular, is crowding the shopping malls. Leaving behind the temples and cultural arenas, they are instead thronging more and more into department stores. Everywhere, people are talking on mobile phones, sending SMS, listening to music, or watching videos on handheld gadgets, thus reminding the older generation that the world has entered a new era, called the digital age.

Those who are religious and cannot cope with these developments are eagerly waiting for doomsday to come. The poor and illiterate who fail to find ways to take part in this competitive world, where money is the most important asset for success, are praying more and more to Heaven and hoping for the Almighty to come to their rescue.

In the first few chapters of this book, I have explained how we have arrived at this stage of social-political evolution following the days of industrialization and colonialism. I have described the important elements of history, which may help readers to understand why things are as they are now, and how one may affect the course of history, by changing the emphasis on which the modern civilization is based.

The world seems to have reached a point of crisis by lacking values and the meaning of life. Scientific knowledge and the success of technology have further added to this moral crisis. The evolutionary theories based on the success of species through competition, dominate mainstream academic thinking, which influences economic theories also. Moreover, the creation theory of the universe, such as the 'Big-Bang', has spread deep roots that destroy the ground meaning that no faith and spiritual nature can grow there anymore. Creation is believed to have been a meaningless accident. With that, the existence of life is also considered as accidental and equally meaningless.

The book is a departure from the above-mentioned mainstream theory of creation, and instead focuses on the nature of our consciousness with which we project our will in the world and shape history.

While rejecting the main stream view about the universe and our mind, I build on an ethical ground, which springs from a new understanding of the universe that is purposeful and follows an eternal design[1]. In the chapter about the source of values, I expand on the nature of the mind, which is deeply connected to the "cosmic-mind" representing a state of consciousness only attainable at a higher-stage of evolution beyond the animal nature. Thus, this book is built on new paradigms regarding the nature of the universe and the mind. These new understandings provide the source of values on which a moral foundation of an enlightened world can be built.

In the second half of the book, I explain what is meant by enlightenment, and how this enlightenment can be achieved through education, creativity, reflection and contemplation. I propose a way by which the present-day democracy could be replaced by a higher form of democracy, which I have called the "Enlightened Democracy".

In the end, I have fancied about a model involving "Civic-organs" which may replace the ideas of the parties that are the basis of present-day democratic systems. The success of building such "Civic-organs" will, in turn, require the existence of an "Enlightened Education and

1 See "Timelessness in Time - A Journey Through a Designed Universe" by Anup Rej, Books of Existence, Oslo, 2014.

15

Culture", which should be imparted to children and youth at an early age.

The purpose of this book is to create a seed from which an enlightened world may spring one day. However, it will require a long process of thinking, discussion and the exchange of ideas amongst people who share the ideas of enlightenment described here, before it can be brought to life.

I hope that this work will initiate a journey to bring human evolution to the path of the "Cosmic-Man" to rebuild our civilization based on the higher-nature of ourselves.

Chapter 1

DYNAMICS BEHIND SOCIAL-POLITICAL ORDER

Evolution of Man

Living things are characterized by their abilities to survive by consuming material available in their environments while assembling highly complex structures from simpler elements available in the surrounding. They have the abilities to replicate themselves and grow by using intelligent methods, where many assembly-line types of works are done in the process of this replication. They can move, motivated by the necessity of survival, reproduction and growth, without being commanded by external forces, or carried by other entities. This is absent in the nonliving world. A nonliving object does not move unless acted upon by external forces, or cannot grow and multiply by assembling simpler structures into highly complex forms. They are not able to choose to act, which can resemble intelligence seen in the living organisms.

However, most plants do not wander around in search for grounds for survival, reproduction and growth. They make use of the conditions available locally in the environment and seek the best strategy to secure their needs of supply of nutrition and energy within the conditions where they grow their roots. They respond to the changing climate and orient themselves according to the ways their existence can be best secured. Their choices arise more as responses to the changing external climate, in which they are destined to live. In contrast, in the animal kingdom the choices are more than mere responses to natural state of affairs. In pursuit of better ground for nutrition, and energy and security for survival and reproduction, they constantly choose their environment defying the rigid ground which tries to destine and control their existence. This indicates a sort of will, which one may call the will-to-live. However, as long as their mobility is constrained within a sphere, they are also destined by the conditions available in that sphere. Higher the mobility and greater the intelligence to make best use of the available resources, more successful the animals become in their struggle for survival and growth.

This freedom to move and choose is invariably threatened by competitions posed by others who are similarly seeking their grounds of survival and security. In a situation where there are not enough resources to sustain and secure all, who desire to live in the same environment, the life becomes an arena of conflict. The primary method of resolving conflicts in the animal kingdom is often the use of brutal physical power. Normally one, who is physically stronger, will win over their weaker competitors. Conflicts also inspire innovation and creativity. By making intelligent use of the brains in newer ways one may be able to find strategies and methods to secure oneself against the dominance of the physically stronger animals. Thus by using creative intelligence one can prevail, like the homo-sapiens has succeeded against the ferocious animals in the jungle.

However, creativity does not bring an end to competition. Rather it can, inspire fiercer competition among the members of the same group. Once one fails to secure one`s ground for survival by one`s own initiative alone, the best strategy is to form a social network of cooperation with others living in a similar situation. This can give a stronger ground to stand against those who may threaten one's existence. The efforts of the many, while sharing methods and means, which have been proved successful and exchanging knowledge and experience, one can greatly enhance the security of life. Most animals develop their own social modes of interactions, which are aimed at this goal.

The animal species, which have been able to secure the desired ground by using creative means and social networking and cooperation, carry urges to maintain their dominance over the less successful species. The fear of losing the secure ground often motivates one to dominate over others. If the dominance goes unchallenged, the successful groups tend to extend their sphere of security even further than what the immediate conditions may demand. Thus they may become more power hungry and develop future strategies to perpetuate their hold of power
.

In this social environment cultures evolve. One may define culture as an intelligent creative way of forging common platforms of cooperation among individuals. By sharing a common view, or forging cooperation around a common social endeavour, or communicating emotional elements appealing to the common nature of the group, who live in similar environment, bonds of cultural cohesion are formed. This is a sphere of interaction which is solely reserved for the human beings. Culture is also a means to develop strategy, acquire knowledge and invent ways to forge social platform where individuals can share their creative possibilities, which may be appreciated by others and made use of by others in order to establish our identity of the group.

With evolution of man, the cultures have diversified. Many different innovative approaches and ideas have created many different cultural groupings. An individual culture can be identified by the knowledge of the world and nature which its members share, and the views about the creation and meaning of life they subscribe to. The fears about the natural catastrophes and the uncontrollable destiny bringing death, unleashed by the natural forces, have led human beings to speculate about a world outside the realm where they live and compete. This has inspired imagination to believe in the existence of supernatural world inhabited by supernatural beings. Often the fears about the supernatural world and the curiosity to understand the dynamics which drive natural phenomena around have resulted in forging a cultural platform. The belief that the supernatural powers can be appeased and invoked to intervene on behalf of a group in order to secure success in the competition against its rivals, has a strong appeal in most cultures. Rituals are prescribed to seek blessings of the supernatural power to fight against others. Societies have thus two main pillars for ensuring securities – one is the military strategists who execute powers in affairs under human control, and the other is the representatives of Heaven, who can call for the intervention of supernatural power to act in one`s favor. Thus most social and cultural diversifications have taken place according to the military-strategic constellation and the spiritual-religious institutions which promise security to the members adhering to the culture. In early days of human civilization, often some living mortal represented Heaven, like the Faraos in Egypt, who ruled in the name of the gods. The military men were amalgamated with the spiritual world, or spiritual representatives became subservient to the military men.

With the passage of history there had been power struggles between the military men defending the society against external threats of power, and the religious men defending the mortals from the wraths of the gods by conducting rituals to appease Heaven.

Historical Background

History has seen evolution of many religious constellations and the tribal and ethnic conglomerations seeking methods of ensuring self-defence, security and searching dominance over other groups. The main keys to success have been the military advantage against the opponents by using knowledge and innovative technological know-how. Cultures have taken shapes, evolved and diversified following power struggles: Ideas have taken new branches; heaven has become "multicoloured". With rising military competence of diverse groups power sharing among them has become a political necessity and the strategy of forming alliance has become pivotal to success.

The history, which has preceded the modern time, is basically a history of ethnic and religious conflicts, where cultural belonging to particular ideologies and views has played central roles. Military advantages and strategic alliances to achieve the military goals have been the way to win and subjugate. Military success has given control over resources and means of exploitations of the vanquished. Thus one`s success has been the loss of freedom for others.

Modern Time: The Globalized World

What is the modern time? When did it begin? And what are the particular characters of this time which is unique in history? How do the historical conditions at present time restrict and condition the evolution of man? How should we try to recondition it and reshape it in order to fulfil the ambition of evolving towards the stage of a "higher-man"?

The definition of modern time will be the point of history when industrialization started in the world, and the world got divided into the two-groups of nations: one enjoying economic advancement due to industrialization and the other succumbing into poverty, injustice, exploitation and colonial dominance by the rising industrial nations. It began with the unprecedented advancement of science and technology, which facilitated production, transport of goods and labor force at large distances from homeland. It brought economic hegemony of a few nations over the rest who had no access to the scientific knowledge and technology. Equipped with the power of innovation and technology, they colonized nations in order to gain control of resources of raw materials and cheap workplace. With rising scientific knowledge and technology, the disparities as regards military power increased in an accelerated speed, which brought the world under knees of a handful of Western nations. The greed for power and wealth of these economically more successful nations generated economic systems of exchange of more abstract nature, which produced values out of "nothing", which could be lent out to debtors who had fallen in economic difficulties. These debts generated even more monetary values out of "nowhere". The world turned into a Devil's Casino and a paradise of wealth and prosperity for a few and a hell of poverty-stricken life for the majority in the world.

The modern banking system introduced abstract ideas, which in essence, became a way of generating capital out of "no production", "no work"….. Simply "nothing", and thus strengthened platform of repressive political and economic systems in the world since the nineteenth century. This monetary system also became a way of grabbing valued properties, once the debtors could not return the debt with interests back in due time. Above all these odds, the colonizing powers introduced taxation systems, which became another ploy of the Devil. Not only the disparities between rich and poor nations increased, but also the social systems which fuel exploitation and grab for properties increased the class differences inside the colonized nations. The collaborators of the colonial powers in the local societies found their "stage of history" as opportune moment to accumulate wealth and grab properties from their own fellow citizens.

Moreover, using the point of supremacy of the colonial power the Western European nations, took to the means of introducing Western values and cultures in their colonies. It brought waves of cultural transformations where the Western culture was viewed by the elites as the desired transformation the societies should follow. The man possessing economic power, who also harnessed most political power, decided the premise of the new cultural development in the society. It shook the cultural arena already being transformed under stress due to improvisation, and precolonial migrations and conquests. Thus it set pace of rapid changes in the pre-industrialized economic and cultural system based on feudalism.

The rapid development and expansion of banking and investments in the industrial productions, meant to bring high profits, set the stage of the modern time. Parallel to the scientific innovations, banking growth, and expansion of the economy to the colonies, the new ideology of capitalism grew. Its proponents saw in this ideology the best way to preserve and serve the cause of human freedom. It was the philosophy of private ownership of the means of production, profits, savings and rights to operate in the economic sector without any intervention from anyone.

It was argued that the mutual agreement between the employers and the laborers about wages and the price, and production of goods based on demand will be the best way to safeguard human freedom. Capitalist philosophy was pivoted on the idea of ownership and the possibility of making maximum profits by using cheap labour. These profits were reinvested to create more profits and thus accumulate more wealth. The collusion between the greedy bankers and the capitalist class changed dramatically the dynamics of the modern civilization.

The servitude of the mass to the feudal class was now replaced by the slavery of the workers under their capitalist employers. This economic bonanza made the Western hemisphere the region of political and economic power of the world. However, capitalist power did not remain in the hand of one country. Several western nations, where industrialization advanced quickly, competed with each other, for money, investment, market and labour.

These competitions soon generated the seeds of world wars and rise of the contending ideologies, which came to challenge capitalism.

The exploitations of the workers with long hours of labour and less wages pushing them to live in wretched living conditions led to Russian Revolution. Economic warfare between France and England against Germany became the hidden cause of the First World War. After the war again the world economy boomed as result of speculations and "casino-culture" of making profits from "nothing", which could in turn be turned into industrial assets. It gave rise to the economic crash (the bursting of the bubble), which sent reverberations throughout the world. It ended up in the rise of Nazism and Fascism in Germany and Italy respectively. The idea of "Superman" and strong state who would guide people to come out of the miseries gained ground. They clashed with the capitalism which saw intervention of state in economic affairs as detrimental to human freedom and synonymous to evil. The rising conflicts of ideologies gave rise to the Second World War when Hitler and Mussolini declared war against France and England. The communists joined the fray. World saw brutality of unprecedented scale on the European soil. Finally with the help of the United States, France and

England and the Capitalist World came out as victorious from the war.

After the demise of Nazism and Fascism, the communism gained in strength and spread its power across Eastern Europe and parts of Asia. With the weakening of the capitalist forces in England and France in a post-world war era, US came out as a fan-bearer of capitalism and the Super-power of the world. Its only enemy became the communists, who increased its military strengths to counter balance the US hegemony. During this period of geo-political competitions, many colonies became independent and free. This generated a new chapter in the evolution of history in the modern World. State controlled socialism competed with capitalism as rival political ideology in the newborn post-colonial states. This challenge to capitalism brought world to the edge of "Cold War" where both sides increased their nuclear arsenals and intercontinental ballistic missiles which could be delivered on the opponents. The fear of nuclear annihilation of Earth gripped the world. The United Nations was formed to safeguard the security of the world, and bring justice in the World System divided into extremely rich part of humanity exploiting the rest of the world living in poverty and dismay. To gain power in the world became synonymous with gaining technological know-how which had remained a monopoly in the hands of the West.

The newly freed colonial states needed money, investment and technology from outside for the development of their economy. The capitalists kept their hegemony by controlling and manipulating this flow. They established World Bank and International Monetary Fund to the cause of development (World Bank is presided by the US citizen while France led IMF). The development aid became a political strategy of the capitalists to contain the march of the communists in the poor parts of the world.

After the Second World War, the communication and media rose as the way of spreading propaganda messages to people with a hope to win their confidence in one, or the other ideology Capitalists emphasized on the freedom of the individuals, while the socialists stressed on the rights of the people and benefits of state control in securing the basic needs of people in the poorer nations. Satellite technology was introduced to spread its stated messages to the remote corners of the world with the help of radio and television.

This media revolution opened up new economic frontiers. The capitalist class started investing in the radio and television industry. It became the easiest way to reach the maximum number of consumers across the globe. The mushrooming of radio and TV channels brought a new dimension to political and economic control and thus maintaining hegemony of the capitalist ideology. The power of money brought power of advertisement and strength to manipulate the views of the less informed population of the world. With it, the windows of the consumption industry opened up to the mass. To keep capitalism alive one needed to generate demand from the population. While the poor could not consume the high-priced luxury goods, they were offered the enjoyment of mass entertainments like sports, crime movies and soap operas etc. Media now entered the economic and political game of the nations, being contested by different ideologies. Film-stars, sport-heroes, media magnets and entertainment show managers started becoming politicians. More fun, more "drink-and-dance", and more private and obscene movies, pictures and stories brought more profits. The world was left to follow the capitalist principles of supply and demand and exploit opportunities which could bring monetary profits as the final goal.

In the face of the glittering advertisement, entertainment and media show of the capitalists against the backdrop of the state controlled propaganda TV of the communist and socialist countries, while their showcases of the consumer goods were nearly empty, the capitalist philosophy of individual freedom triumphed. With it the bastions of socialism and communism gave way to the methods of the capitalists. The communist nations too adopted the free-market mechanism. This opening brought more monetary flow and investment from the capitalist countries and generated economic development in an accelerated pace.

When Soviet Union collapsed in the early 90s and lost its grip of power over the countries in the Eastern Europe, the newly freed countries rushed to join the Capitalist club. By then the nations of Western Europe, who had waged two World Wars in the first half of the 20th century, in order to avoid any world war in the European soil in the future had formed a union. Some of the freed Eastern European states were given membership to this union (first created by France and Germany).

The rapid growth of economics in Asia (which once fell back), as a result of rearrangements which had taken place since the end of the Second World War, and due to new economic strategies of the former socialist and communist states, the supply to the market of the consumer goods in Europe and America increased in leaps and bounds. It brought the "live the life" lifestyle for the people in the richer world, while people in the others nations worked and produced. With the increased free time and wealth in the hands of the common people in the West, the tourism and travel industry boomed. Much of the tourism destination moved towards Asia, contributing to the rise of tourism as important contributor to the economic growth of some of these countries. Capitalists quickly moved to exploit this opportunity.

The spending spree on consumer articles, entertainment, travel and leisure by the rich is now generating growth in economics of the poorer nations too. The world economy is getting more and more globalized, where economic downturn in one part of the world have consequences for the rest.

In this economy of consumer culture the central factor is the level of consumption. Until industrialization, the main energy source was bio-matter, like wood and cow-dung. After industrialization coal became the dominating energy source. After the Second World War, the increased fleets of automobiles and air crafts have changed demand for the main energy source to oil. The increased urbanization, fast expansion of markets, and needs for transports to keep the chain of demand and supply in balance, in order to avoid economic crisis, is adding in polluting the environment. The air in big cities is becoming hazardous for health. Apart from that, some believe that the present economic system is contributing to the possibility of extinction of the human race. By burning fuels in larger and larger amounts every year, in order to run the industries, which keep the production chains going, and using vehicles transporting people and goods in even larger numbers, the pace of development is contributing in changing the natural climate on Earth. Many believe that by emitting gases, which develop from burning the fuels, we have already changed the climate pattern, which may have dire consequences as regards the survival of many species, including the human beings. The luxury of consumption and flights of leisure and pleasure (as one feels free to do), is making our chances for survival on Earth less and less in the long run. Capitalism in fact can mean a death-trap for mankind. Already there are signs of the danger as observed in the erratic weather patterns including hurricanes, floods and droughts of unusual character all around the globe.

The evil of the capitalist culture of consumption may have already slipped out of hand. While more and more people in the West is going over to bicycles (in order not to pollute the environment), the production of automobiles are increasing fast in the developing countries. In a country like China the demand for oil is soon going to reach the level in the West. The slowing down of economics in the West is being compensated by the fast economic growth rate in Asia. People call it as an "Asian Era", where China and India are the main motors driving the World economy. Both are pursuing the free-market track in order to keep up a fast rate of growth, while the Banking and monetary system are still running in the same old capitalistic way.

The essential elements, on which the success of the economic competition hinges on today, is the availability of energy resources-particularly oil. The geopolitical game behind economic and political success in the future appears to be the success in controlling and securing the energy resources. The political success of ideologies depends on the economic success in securing work, income, property and health services to people.

It appears that the capitalism as an ideology is losing its steam in the Western countries. The increased standard of living condition and demand for luxury of living are making the availability of the labour-force more and more scarce in the West. Everybody wants to enjoy life and no one wants to work in the industries reminiscent of the past capitalistic mode. In Western Europe, more and more labour forces are coming from the newly freed Eastern Europe, who has lagged behind in economic development due to the control of the region by the Communist Soviet Union. High labour prices and costs of providing the social facilities, which the workers are entitled to in the west, are making the investors to look to Asia, in particular, for success. There the labor is cheap and responsibility to provide social benefits to the workers can be easily avoided. In this way the capitalists are making other nations as their breeding grounds outside the traditional dens, where industrialization once started. Multinationals are spreading their umbrellas wherever there are possibilities of profits one may make. Through establishing monopolies in the market they advertise themselves as the defender of human freedom. They argue that man and woman can now freely choose and consume according to their mental make ups and taste. With it the values in Asia is also changing. Now the motto of life is becoming: "Earn money, buy and enjoy". The rise of the Asian economy coincides with the rise of the internet cultures, including social networking, which is becoming more and more a cyber market of advertisement. Economic competitions have started looking into those places too, as potential grounds to explore for success. People leave their personal information related to their choices of consumption articles and nature of entertainments they prefer. Here people are also lured in leaving information about their political belief and philosophy of life, among others. These information are accessible for business class to freely analyse and then decide strategies to entrap customers for buying their products.

With it, the investments are increasing in great speed in technologies related to delivering the social network of entertainment and advertisement of hand-held gadgets like mobile phones and tablets. The grip of the capitalist world is becoming more and more sinister and invisible. Computers can crunch out data and see patterns of social behaviours much more easily than it was possible any time before. Moreover, it can do it in no time. By looking at the existing social patterns and trends one can further inculpate in degrading humanity to choose a path of downfall as an "economic animal of consumption". While the educated and the wise population of the West, who is weary of capitalist values, have started discovering this sinister development, the population in the parts of the world, where consumer culture is new, the temptation and danger of being swept by this economic ploy appears very high.

Not only the new technology is offering "freedom" to the young generation to chat, make fun, exchange private information with the world at no-cost, it is also playing its role as a mediator in the political evolution of the world in the 21st century.

Televisions, radio, newspapers, governmental and non-governmental organizations, artists, businessman or anyone who has anything to sell, advertise or promote anything to a larger invisible community in the world, are all joining this "social revolution". In return of giving people the opportunity to chat and exchange private photographs and thoughts, or invite strangers to one's private shows (which may include art works, grimace, scenes of violence or sex), the new generation is delivering their future in the hands of the money-makers, who know no other goal but making profits.

This cyber technology is also being used in the game of winning competitions in the geopolitical struggle for power. Social networking is being used in organizing movements against governments and political opponents. An organized small group has the possibility to send information including graphics and videos over the net in a lightning speed and multiply the recipients of the information in an exponential way. These are mostly being used in defence of "democracy and freedom" - of course, supporting the interests of the capitalist class. Most recently the dynamics of political upheaval in the Arab World is maintained by this cyber revolution. Channelling information, which carry much misinformation, and give propaganda advantage against the governments, or opponents to be thrown, are becoming effective instruments for the countries promoting their interests by using the slogan of "human rights and freedom".

By creating mass-protests which would be inevitably answered by violent means by the governments, the cyber revolution is being used to create public opinion in the world in support of military intervention by the West. In the face of competition and rising power of China and Asia, who side with Russia to try to curb the Western hegemony of economic and political dominance,West is inventing new strategies to intervene wherever its economic and political interests could be in danger. This is, at present, the case in Syria and Iran, two powerful countries in the Middle East, who may decide the geopolitical destiny of the West. This geopolitical crisis is arising due to the competitions for access to oil and gas supply and its control. The winners in the region will have advantage in deciding the premises of the economic and political developments in the world in the near future.

The new revolutions in the Middle East are being instigated on the issues of age old religious rivalries among different religious factions in Islam - particularly the Shias and the Sunnis. It is the old technique of the Western powers, which they have used in the past. The geopolitical battle with the desire of holding the age old political and economic hegemony of the West is bringing unprecedented brutality and suffering on the people in the region.

In an atmosphere of violence and chaos, more fundamentalist jihadist groups, a lá Al-Qaida, are surging and coming in the forefront. The rise of this murderous force is freeing the power who wishes to get rid of the capitalist system, which, as a contradiction of history, is opening up the gates for their own demise. Thus the world is getting embroiled into multiple levels of complexities and becoming more and more confusing to understand.

What the future may bring is not clear. However, the economic glooms in the West and the political chaos in the oil-rich Arab countries point to a wearisome scenario for the near future. The stock-market crash in 2007, which resembled the one which occurred a decade before the World War II, and the long-lasting economic crisis plaguing the countries of the Euro-zone these days indicate that a major change must occur in the world before the world order can get out of the mess in which it has got embroiled.

The social economic conditions of different countries in the world are reflecting this situation of history at the verge of taking a new turn: Here more than a billion of people are still buried under the poverty line of one dollar a day, without access to water, education and nutrition. Even after the economic growths in Asia, hundreds of millions of people are extremely poor in India and China (not to mention the less successful countries).

Chapter 2
SECURITY OF LIFE UNDER DIFFERENT ECONOMIC AND POLITICAL SYSTEMS

Economic System

Economic system embodies access to resources supporting the conditions of survival like food, shelter and security against threats to life caused by changes in environments, and social instabilities. The system ensures modes of production of goods and services beneficial for the community which ensure security and survival of the members sharing the system. It is often based on ownership rights to properties, which are basis of food production and provide ground for building shelters and settlements. Economic system prescribes the way the rights to possession of resources and means of production are distributed among the members of the society. Every economy assigns values to the objects people need, according to the availability of the objects and the labor involved in bringing them to the market for consumption by others. Values originate from practices in the market, which can be either coercive, or free. Free exchange is possible when the parties, exchanging good, enjoy parity of powers to defend self-interest, and values of one's labor and innovation. When one side suffers from dire needs and extreme conditions of survival, the other side, that may enjoy abundance of resources and are in a position to exploit weaknesses of the others, may downgrade the values of the objects and labour, which the weaker partners provide. Thus a system of exploitation can be instituted.

To avoid the growth of such exploitative mechanism, one needs consensus about what is economic justice that can secure just values to different objects and services provided by different individuals in the community? As long as human beings operate as actors in the market as individuals seeking advantages, profits and more security for oneself at the expense of other's security of life, there is no other way to define justice above the principle of "might is right". Only the realization that one's security and quality of life depends on the security and quality of life of others can set the premise of justice where exploitations can be avoided. Love, compassion and solidarity are the foundations of such a just society.

Many argue that love and compassion are not too natural to human species: Human beings are propelled by self-interests and desire of possessing resources advantageous to oneself and the ones nearest to him/her. Sharing with the community as an equal member is not the natural instinct of man. Possession, control and dominance are more natural to our specie. Self-fulfillment is a greater drive for man to act than contributing to the welfare of others.

This philosophy and view of life have driven the modern capitalism. Prior to the rise of industrial capitalism, accumulation of landed properties in the hands of a few, while the majority lived by selling their labor and products as agricultural workers, defined the feudal economic mode. In such a feudal system the values were based on scarcity or abundance, and the needs of the population for particular goods or services. They possessed a character of more informal exchange. The feudal lords could generate wealth by methods of taxations and setting up hegemonic authorities over landed properties. When those feudal lords did not distribute wealth for redressing the improvement of livelihood of people, and instead improvised the population, they were considered despotic.

These despots maintained their hegemonies of power by supporting clans and militia, who gained benefits for their loyalties. Organizing military power became a way of defending unjust systems. The political organizations evolved out of this process. In the evolution of the social justice, the religious groups took major roles in the feudal economy. Religious institutions, promoting an ethical view of justice, derived from religious scriptures or doctrines, became the competitors of the military despots. These religious men too built their power of influence over the agricultural resources, and labour. In the name of justice coming from Heaven, they amassed wealth and power, while the laity sank into misery, ignorance and superstitious beliefs.

Thus economics, politics and religions became interlinked and took institutionalized forms supporting different forces. Religion brought ethical foundation, while aligning itself to the exploitative mechanism of the despotic political rulers. The political organizations developed defences of economic systems by military means. The ordinary people, who produced and supplied goods to the markets, became more and more helpless actors, who had to accept the values dictated by their masters.

Supportive elements of an economic system

Every economic system has several supporting pillars which consist of different institutional mechanisms: The political mechanism helps to defend and secure the economic zone in which it operates. It is supported by military power whose success hinged on military-technological know-how. It also governs the distribution and control of means of production and availability of labours for different production sectors.

Thus an economic system is not any isolated enterprise of the society separate from political system, defence, education, communication and transport, and legal institution which ensures security and justice. In a healthy social-order, these pillars remain stable and can bring comfort and trust between those who invest and those who assure the functioning of the different elements supporting the economic life.

The efficient functioning of the market, where people can exchange goods and services depends on the development of means of communication and transport, and thus relies on the presence of a social structure which can build and maintain these infrastructures.

Then there are needs for rules of conduct in the market, which may build trust among people who exchange goods and services.

The sustainability of the market including production, distribution and consumption depend on the willingness of the people to produce, exchange and consume.

The production chains cannot be maintained without availability of raw-material, and labour force and the source from where wages can be paid and raw-materials can be purchased. Initial investment to finance the production in the form of money is an essential aspect of this mechanism behind sustainability of an economy.

The economy may fail in the lack of expertise and knowledge needed to generate the goods and services. It needs a steady infusion of innovation in order to increase the growth rate and ameliorate the working conditions of the workers. Knowledge and education are the backbones for sustaining a healthy economic growth and building environments in which the workers may feel content and motivated.

The society, which can accommodate justice and bring more freedom and comfort to the majority of the population and avoid confrontations and conflicts by infusing knowledge and education to people about the way harmony and peace may be established, becomes a more successful society.

Different economic systems

Economic system which embodies different aspects of social order, as mentioned above, needs a governing authority for its functioning. The governing authority, acting on behalf of the people, decides the legal premises, defends the economic interests by employing military means, and facilitates building infrastructures and educational and learning institutions, and stimulates investments, employments etc. There exist various ideas about how the state should govern, and what would be the visions and values which should guide the state in acting and forming a social-economic order. Who should sanction the state to build nation on some ideas instead of others, which it should be able to defend as the right way of governing the people?

In earlier time many kings/emperors had assumed the authority by declaring themselves as the representatives of Heaven and God. They made people believe that through their mediation the Divine plans were manifest in the world. In more primitive societies, the persons claiming the power of magic and connecting to the spirit world had taken the role of being the moderator between the invisible world and the life on Earth. The imagined Heaven or the invisible spirit world was the realm which provided the rulers with the authority to shape and build communities and states according to their whims. Thus religious beliefs had played central roles in the pre-scientific age. Many despots, who could organize military means to conquer and subjugate people with power, allied with religious leaders, often conferred upon themselves authorities and rights to rule. The people's fear of the power of Heaven, existing outside the sphere of the mortals living on Earth, had been utilized in promoting ideas in building states.

In the traditional agriculture based society kings and religious men distributed among themselves the authorities to enact laws, organize institutions, and employ people in economic activities.

The growth of trade across nations and particularly the success of the western merchants in colonizing large parts of the world, brought changes in this order which was once "organized" between Heaven and Earth. Merchants rose to carve in their power base in the social-economic sphere without asking for sanctions of the traditional actors. Then industrialization came. The power of the bankers and traders grew, who began to assert themselves more and more over heavenly and kingly powers. When capitalism became the "mode operandi" of the society, capitalists allied themselves to the religious forces to gain greater acceptance of the people about their roles as extended hands of the state.

The alliance of the religious leaders, capitalists and the feudal lords came to be challenged by the rising power of the intellectuals and scientific minded people, who understood the falsity of Heaven and the conspiracy of the ruling class to keep the mass in chains. The socialist revolutions began. Marx declared religion as the opium of the people and professed a "scientific" theory of history on the basis of the philosophy of dialectical-materialism. It builds on the idea that history, at every juncture, develops contradictions and conflicts, which lead to new contradictions and conflicts once the old contradictions are resolved. These contradictions arise from the material nature of the world and its laws. According to the Marxists there is no Heaven and God behind the movements of historical development of the human societies. The material conditions and conflicts of interests and method to produce livelihood and control of the community by different means, decide the evolution of history.

The socialist revolution, which brought private properties under state control, and emphasized about the good of the community and freedom of the working class as a priority in social development, was followed by the peasant revolution in China, known as "Maoist revolution". It set as its goal to eliminate the traditional cultural elements in the society, which have conspired to keep the mass in chains. It attacked temples and learning centres which taught about the heavenly way and the power of the rulers derived from Heaven. Peasants were equipped with guns to bring changes in the old order. Properties were confiscated; the class enjoying pleasure and leisure were sent to fields to tilt; and communes were established to provide food, health, shelter and justice to the oppressed. Those, who once remained prisoners of the proprietor class, took over the power of deciding over their own destinies, under the leadership of the Communist Party. Atrocities and bloodshed followed.

In contrast, the capitalist social-order emphasized on the private ownership of properties and means of production and the "sanctity of the free-market" which was driven by the supply and demand. The philosophy of making profits and thus generating wealth, which further could be invested to make more profit and wealth, drove the dynamics of accumulation of wealth and property. The belief, that without such interests in making one's fortune, the human beings would not engage in economic development of the society, was accepted as a natural behaviour of human kind. Human beings, in this system, were seen as economic animals, who preyed on each other to compete, survive and dominate.

The role of the state in the capitalist system was to guarantee the security of the free-market economy and thus promote the individual freedom of greed. Laws were meant to secure private ownership and preventing others in trespassing one's private sphere.

Democracy and human rights became important slogans in this system. Human rights often meant the rights of the individuals in participating freely in shaping the socioeconomic sphere. In countries where the capitalism won unchallenged position, the power of democracy was defended against any authority in deciding over the affairs of the people. While the people remained enchained in production and consumption, the religion provided the ideology in support of the capitalistic freedom. Moreover, these capitalist nations acted from a "higher" ground of military and technological advantages over other nations and people. By supporting the democratic system which provided such advantages, the people of the democratic nations found ways to maintain their hegemony over the rest of the world. The people of these democratic nations comprising of a small percentage of the population of the world continued consuming the largest chunks of all resources in the world.

Democracy and human rights became instruments for the capitalist nations to tear down the power of the challengers who tried to create any socialist or communist states. India, the crown in the British Colony, became the "biggest democracy" of the world - a democracy of the poverty stricken illiterate population, which could be easily manipulated along caste and religious lines. Along with it, the age-old feudal culture cast its shadow in a democracy where caste and class divisions of extreme poor and extreme rich had remained the greatest evil of the modern time.

In countries which lay in the peripheries of the main industrialized nations in the West, where primary economy was substantive, a mixed economy evolved like in Scandinavia. The lack of manufacturing industries seeking outside market and absence of colonial privileges to infiltrate markets of other countries left these nations to develop a less exploitative economy. Though capitalism entered, it was brought under some government control – a sort of socialism that instead of generating an extremely rich class favoured the development of welfare of the mass, .

Socialism and Communism making roads for Capitalism

The main ideas challenging the capitalism were the socialism and Maoism, which came into life in the twentieth century. Socialism professed the idea of the ownership of the means of production, and the power of distribution of profits in the hands of the workers. With it the financial control was left with the state, where the workers played central roles in its governance. While socialism stressed on the necessity to work and produce in order to earn livelihood and enjoy an equal quality of life by sharing the fruits of production, the communism went a step further. It professed the idea of a society where everybody would receive what they needed for living - not necessarily based on the amount of labour provided by the individuals. It was an idea of a utopian world.

Marx believed that the capitalistic mode of production and exploitation would alienate human beings, who would revolt and the workers will finally take over the control of the means of production, and the control of fair wage payment in their own hands. He argued that the demise of capitalism was inevitable in history – like a law of nature. In his view the contradiction brought by capitalism, as a system of freedom where only a few enjoyed the luxuries of life in leisure and pleasure at the cost servitude of the mass, would be resolved by the rise of socialism.

In fact, this philosophical idea never materialized. No revolution occurred in the countries where capitalism flourished after industrialization. Instead, socialist revolution took place in a less advanced economy, like in Russia. It was a revolt against Czarist feudal system and exploitations of the labourers in the military industries. The revolution gave birth to a centralized economy controlled by the state. The other revolution took place in China in an agrarian setting suffering from the colonial history. It became a peasants uprising against the propertied class, who utilized the old-age feudal mechanism of exploitation.

The rise of the state control in the socialist and Maoist states resulted in the stop of the flow of any investment from the capitalist countries to the economies of these nations, and consequently brought slow down in the process of industrialization in these poorer nations. At the same time the reconstruction of Europe after the Second World War brought industrial advancements in the West in leaps and bounds. With it the gap between the North and the South increased.

Moreover, the newly independent nations, freed from the colonial powers, took inward looking policies in order to avoid being exploited by their former masters. Some took to authoritarian military rules (authoritarianism and economic growth became synonymous). It became a period of exploitations of the mass by the local elites, keeping ties with the undemocratic setup and methods of the colonial rulers. In this state of transition of the world, the ideas of socialism took various shapes, fitting with the cultural makeup and the historical characters of the nations.

The world got divided into two blocks: Capitalists included some dictatorial rulers of the developing nations, while the socialists appealed to the intellectual class aspiring to free their countries from the hegemonies of the capitalist powers and their support of authoritarian dictators. Soviet Union, which became the leader of the International Socialist movement, became authoritarian in turn, and failed to live up to the aspiration of freedom of the people. Moreover it generated corruptions of power and links between the party bosses and the economic life of state driven production mechanism. The managerial class and the bureaucrats became the new elites of the society, while the workers and the ordinary people became more passive under the socialist development. The state provided the basic housing, health and education, while depriving people of freedoms of expressions and creativity not sanctioned by the state. Socialists propaganda, which failed to bring human development outside the narrow interests of the elites controlled by the party, made such a system stagnant.

Maoism took to violence and oppression of the intellectual and cultural elites of the society based on the idea of creating a nation free from enemies of the peasants. It was a peasant revolution led by armed mass, who saw adherent of other ideologies as enemies of the people. They tried to uproot the nation from its past cultural legacy.

The capitalist nations in the West counteracted this development by putting emphasis on human rights and democracy – particularly, the civil and political rights of the individuals in support of the freedom of belief, faith and view. The socialists and communists stressed on the rights of development of the people – particularly education, food and health facilities for all.

The rising influence of the radio, television and mass media across the globe and the integration of the communication technology across the nations, have exposed to the world the "superiority" of consumer freedom, which the capitalist economy professes, against the meagre consumer life which the socialist system is able to produce. With the power of advertisement the world has been eluded to believe in the type of freedom which lies at the heart of a consumer oriented culture. Socialist Russia and Communist China, together with all others, who once saw freedom in the hands of the state controlled mechanism, have now realized the power of the consumer culture. They have all adopted some form of capitalism, though somewhat different from the Anglo-Saxon Capitalism which one knows from the past. Thus capitalism is reorienting itself into different directions in Russia, China, India and some other Asian and Latin American states. They are being called by different names: Red-Capitalism, Crony-Capitalism, Oligarchic-Capitalism etc.

New capitalistic paths

In the beginning of 1980s China took to capitalist path of its own type. It started in the agricultural production sector and co-operatives. Private ownership in these sectors brought growth. However, this capitalism was governed by the Chinese Communist Party. The party bosses and bureaucrats became the driving force behind the economic model. Under one party dictatorship a policy of economic development in line with capitalistic mode of production and free-market brought accelerated economic development in China. The party, steered by technocrats, businessmen, and bureaucrats adopted unconventional ways of success in the economic development. The laws and rules were adjusted, broken or overlooked in order to achieve the economic target. It brought the global consumer culture to China and with it an unprecedented economic investment by the West in the Chinese economy. Cheap labour and huge disciplined work force brought great advantage to China in exporting goods to the West and accumulating wealth. Now Chinese economy has become so robust that it has started buying in the industrial sector in the West, and becoming a big lender in the international monetary market.

Russia saw the demise of Socialism in the early 1990s. The collapse of the Soviet Union set a new chaotic dynamics in the Russian economy. The shadow economy which was run by mafias during the Soviet era became the leading force in the new capitalistic venture. The party bureaucrats and managers, who always took advantages of their political powers in an authoritarian system, collaborated with the rising economic class in order to get their shares of the economic "looting" of the country. The foreign investors joined the fray and added their contributions in the chaotic development of the economy. Mafia links, criminal practices and abuse of connections to power elites created new Russian oligarchs in the post Soviet Union. The attempts to bring order in this corruption and chaos by authoritarian means were counteracted with the demand for human rights, democracy and individual freedom, supported and financed by the Western capitalists. It became a golden opportunity for them to dismantle a power structure which had ability to threaten capitalist world with military means.

In India, the socialism of Indian kind, introduced by Nehru after independence, gave rise to capitalism of Indian style. It started in the early years of 1990s with liberalization and opening up of the economy for investment. By then India has been freed from its Socialist ties with the Soviet Union. The demise of the Socialist ideology and state control of the heavy industries, opened India to jump into capitalist path. The IT industries became a way to enter into this capitalist adventure. The huge intellectual work-force of scientists and engineers brought a boom to Indian growth. With the investors from the West- especially the US-Indians - the consumer culture entered India.

However, Indian capitalism took its own route based on the traditional oligarchical and feudal nature of the society. Before that, there was a monolithic structure already laid by a few families dominating the Indian economy. The concentration of huge fortunes in a few hands still characterized the Indian landscape, known for "Maharajas" from the past. Bribes, corruption and overpowering legal systems with powerful political connections became symptomatic of Indian Capitalistic growth.

Amidst this, India runs its "biggest show of democracy in the World". The purpose of this democracy is not to empower people in freeing themselves from a system which bring disparities and inequalities in the society, but to mass mobilize illiterate population to serve the interests of groups, who harness the political forces of the nation. Illiteracy, caste, cheap entertainments supplied by film and TV industries add to the owe of the people. They halt efforts in building a system that may empower the unprivileged and poor to come out of the clutches of the oligarchs of this "Elephant- Capitalism". Privately owned media-channels, which flourish at an increasing rate, vigorously defend this democracy, as path of competition for economic and political powers among the "Oligrach-Capitalists".

In other parts of Asia, like in the ASEAN countries, the capitalism is taking their indigenous shapes according to the precolonial social structure and the dynamics of history brought forth by the conflicts between the capitalist West and the socialist Russia and communist China after the Second World War.

Global economic crisis: Back to Socialism?

In a globalized world investments are moving across countries in search of higher profits, brought by cheaper skilled and unskilled labour forces and availability of raw materials, combined with less government regulations controlling foreign investments. Capitalist's holy mantra is: "Profit and more profit" and create money from nothing by utilizing the mechanism of stock-exchange and dubious banking practices.

The growth of the Asian economies has occurred in parallel with the slowdown of the economics of the Western World. In 2007 the Western economies faced a major crisis due to lack of faith in the banking system bringing a stock-market collapse. It was the biggest financial crisis world had seen since the financial crisis of 1929. It implied the deficiencies of the capitalist economic theories and forced the intervention of the Western Governments to help the free-market economy to come on feet.

Since the economic crisis of 2007, the Western economy is heading towards recession. The biggest economy of the West, the US, is debt ridden. It has incurred debt to the level that warns of a serious repercussion in the future of the world economy. The Euro-zone economy is in turmoil creating huge unemployment and economic dismay in countries like, Greece, Spain, Portugal and Italy. Their economies are being salvaged by the European Central Banks. Free-market mechanism seemed to have lost its dynamics by which, it had survived so long.

It is becoming increasingly clear that a new monetary and financial mechanism must emerge before the world can find economic stability.

In this critical moment, the access to energy-particularly oil- is becoming an important factor as a vital instrument in a new geopolitical battle. So, the fear of war in pursuit of gaining dominance of the oil resources is increasing.

It is quite possible that a conflict around oil resources may start a new World War. The outcome of such a war will decide the framework of a new global economic system.

Different Structures of Governments

Different social systems organized the governance of the state in different ways. The capitalist systems chose the democratic way of participation of wider groups in selecting people who would govern their societies. In newer time, two main form of democratic governance developed: One was the presidential system and the other was the parliamentary democracy. They were based on the way the authorities to rule were prescribed on different persons and bodies.

In the presidential system, the highest authority of power was conferred on the president of the nation, who was chosen by direct election by the people. He/she was the head of the executive body of the state implementing laws and policies. In American (US) presidential system, the structure of governance was divided into three different branches: The Legislative, Executive and Judiciary. The legislative branch passed laws and authorized the executive branch to carry out the laws and policies adopted by the law giving body. The executive branch executed the affairs of the state like food, health, security, financial transaction, education, military etc. The judiciary acted as a watch dog. Their role was to see that no one acted outside the laws of the state. People, through direct election, chose the members of the Senate and the Congress, who would authorize the president to carry out the policies. The president nominated the judges in the Supreme Court. The nominations had to be sanctioned by the Senate. So there existed a check and balance of power among different branches, eliminating the possibility of an autocratic rule.

The election in such a system is mostly a show of media and wealth. The most effective way one may bring the messages to the people decides the outcome of such an election. In this competition only people with high-degree of connections to the financial and media world can survive. People with military background, or financial tycoons have often succeeded in such a system. Religious faiths also colour the election results.

Such democratic system had grown out of a more traditional system, where religious men, traders and businessmen and kings and feudal lords had played major roles in the sociopolitical development of nations.

The other form of democratic political system is the parliamentary system, where the head of the state is either a monarch or a president, who play mostly ceremonial role without any real power in their hands. The power lies in the hands of the members of the parliament, who are directly elected by the people. This form of democracy, which has its strongest roots in the Western Europe, promotes fairer competitions of interests and ideas, which are not overwhelmed by financial and military ties. Such a system stimulates more vigorous participations of parties bearing different ideologies. The elected parties (can be a coalition of several parties) choose a prime minister to run the affairs of the nation. The prime minister chooses a cabinet of ministers, who get executive powers to implement the policies which the parties have advocated during the election. Election commissioner supervises election process, to make sure that elections do not become fraudulent and power is not snatched by any party by illegal means.

In the beginning, this form of parliamentary system was based on elections where the privileged people were mostly allowed to vote. The privileges included the wealth and property one possessed, and the military and religious power one could harness. In India, this parliamentary system was introduced by the British as a method of the British crown to curb the influence of the British traders who had monopoly of power. However, at this time only a handful of people could elect. With the rise of nationalism in India, at the wake of the

First World War, the franchises were extended to the rich and power-ful people of the country. The universal suffrage was granted only after independence.

However, in a traditional society, where religion and caste played central roles in forming the social-order, the election became a ground to be manipulated by the feudal class. In a society plagued by poverty, illiteracy and inequalities, the methods to mobilize the mass to vote for people enjoying traditional power, followed the behaviour of a feudal society, stooped deeply in religious faith.

The other main political systems which took their roots in the twentieth century were socialism and communism. They refuted the ideas of the Western-led democracies, which became instruments of the powerful and wealthy to come to power, while the mass lived in insecurities and ignorance. The idea of transferring power to the hands of those who worked in the factories or tilled the lands became central in socialist and communist system. After the Russian Revolution, the workers formed Soviets i.e. units of power at the grass root level that comprised of members elected by the workers and peasants. Only the workers and peasants were allowed to elect the representatives. The others, who were seen as the enemies of the proletariat class, remained disfranchised until very late in the 1970s, when a new constitution allowed the other classes in the society to participate in elections.

The Soviets in the grass root level sent representatives to the higher level, which in turn sent representatives to even higher level, and so on...... finally forming the main legislative and executive power of the nation, dominated by the members of the socialist/communist party. It became a bulldozer system, where the power in the party hierarchy and conformity with the ideologies of the party decided the freedom and possibilities one could enjoy in the social-political arena.

Lenin argued that the workers did not have leisure and opportunities to study and comprehend the complexities of Marxism and the full advantages of the socialist system. They needed guidance by the intellectual elites who wanted to change the social order in favor of the working people. The workers, he said, mostly understood the situation in the immediate working place, and could not bring the vision of the great social change in the national level. The intellectuals guiding the ideologies of the party were supposed to lead the socialist revolution. The involvement in the activities of the party became a way for the intellectuals and middle class to gain political power and assert their interests in the social-order.

The party membership became a way of getting jobs, privileges and access to management in state enterprises. It soon became the corrupt way of using party power to consolidate private interests. Thus the intellectual socialist leaders, in the end, became the cause of downfall of socialism. The workers became passive and were used as tools in the social mobilization.

The story of the communist China followed a different route. Elections were held at the grass root level, where the candidates to be elected were members of the communist party, or needed support of the party for a successful candidacy. The governance was controlled by the local councils in different levels following the ideology of the communist party. The member of the lower level of the council sent representatives to councils at higher levels. At the top the pyramid was the National Council and the politburo. At every level party loyalty determined the success of election, privileges and opening up of the opportunities.

When communist party liberalized its policies, and opened up private enterprises and global partnership with the capitalist West, the party, instead of being a body serving the interests of the peasants and the workers, became a forum for technocrats, intellectuals, military and businessmen. These party bureaucrats, at all levels, created and broke rules by using their political muscles, and created fortunes for themselves, and the people allied with them. It became a laissez-faire capitalism, whose main aim was to produce, invest and make profit by any convenient means suitable to achieve the goal – law, or no-law meant how successfully one could avoid and implement economic success. Corruption became tantamount to such a system. At present, the remnant of communism is only the organization structure of the party and way people are elected at different levels of government. Through this political forum different interests of the society take shape – a very different approach than the democratic West.

Chapter 3
FACES OF DEMOCRACY IN THE WORLD

True democracy is a decision making procedure in an organization or in a governing system which includes the participation of all belonging to the organization, or direct beneficiaries of the system. In a democracy, it is the people, made of individuals, who should enjoy freedom to execute their will and desires in shaping the social, economic and political environment to which one wishes to belong. By enacting a principle of equal rights of participation by all in shaping a common platform of social-political-economic order, which embraces diverging views, the democracy professes a process of forging a life of a social group, who may share and sustain common goods and build a life of peaceful coexistence. The core idea hinges on the primacy of the individual and his/her will and how to tame it in the social context through a participatory process, which may require compromise and dialogue. It is often described by a famous quotation: "Democracy is the government of the people, by the people, for the people."

Everybody is included in the word people: Rich or poor, illiterate or wise; weak or strong; blind and deaf or a genius etc. They are all assumed to have equal rights and responsibilities in shaping the world where one wants to live a meaningful life in harmony and peace. In earlier period of history most people were excluded in decision making over the nature of the social evolution: At that time either the decisions were made by the despots, or by the aristocrats. Only in newer time the idea of realizing democracy has come into vogue.

However in the modern world today people do not represent any homogeneous mass of same race, culture, belief and equal opportunities anywhere. Throughout history the extensive plundering by diverse interest groups encroaching on others` territories and freedom, have left a very inhomogeneous society everywhere. Even in a small local arena people do not enjoy equal means to acquire knowledge, education, economic opportunities of survival etc. In every society all over the world, there exist inequalities and differences. In some places it is so great that different individuals may appear to belong to different world altogether, although they may be living close by each other.

In modern democracy such people with diverse economic opportunities, education, awareness and know-how about technology and science, and living in totally different mental worlds are supposed to forge a common ground on which a governing system can be erected, which will reflect the will of all, and act as a foundation for a peaceful society that all can trust and where everybody may feel secure.

The modern democracy aspires for a majority rule represented by parties possessing different political and social programs. Whatever rules and laws, and views and values promulgated by a party receive most votes, they decide what all must abide by in the society. In a better democracy the governing authority does not try to suppress the competing ideas by using means of power at its disposal, and instead leaves room for the opposing parties to express grievances through protest actions and creating information channels through which new views and ideas may emerge. This form of democracies follow rule of law and abide by the rights of all of the population to enjoy freedom to express and challenge the ideas of the governing party.

Examples of democracy in the real world

However, the way democracies function in the real world is very different from place to place. It is difficult to characterize it in the way the democracy is described above. Here are some examples:

INDIA

In India peoples` participation came after independence from the British rule and formation of a government led by the Congress party. The party was formed by the wealthiest and the most powerful of the Indians, led by Oxford and Cambridge educated people. The party was formed as a sequel of agitation by the wealthy Indians to share power with the British. When the British left, this party of business tycoons, industrialists and zamindars won a landslide victory in poverty stricken and caste-ridden country with over 80% illiteracy at that time. In a country where more than 85% of the population was peasant (1951), the party of the feudal class swept the election. In a democracy of the poor and illiterate the wealthy and rich became the rulers of India. And still now the same family, who ascended to power after independence, rules India.

Of course, the Indian democracy has evolved to reflect the diversity of the ethnic groups, religions and languages, for example. Minorities and Dalits (untouchables) have also found their parties and bases to rise as political forces. Caste, creed, religion etc. have become essential factors for the illiterate and the poor to identify themselves with a party. Different parties too have chosen different policies satisfying the popular needs. Through mushrooming of TV channels and political debates now there exists a heightened awareness among people about the value of the rights to vote in an election. However, there are only a few things which give direction to the democratic process: It is mainly concentrated on the economic and cultural survival in a fiercely increasing competition which has risen with the globalized free market economy. People snatch what they can for their region, caste, creed and family. In this hullabaloo of democracy the dynastic rule of Nehru family continues, and may continue in the future. The feudal mentality still keeps its hold in the Indian mind. Above it, the Indian-American, investing in business in India, is becoming the fuel-burner of the rising technocrat-oriented economy of India. This new class is revamping the glamour of the rich class from where the Congress Party once descended.

BANGLADESH

In Bangladesh, which has come to its existence with the military help of India during independence, the historical context remains the same as in the Eastern India - the place from where British once expanded its rule to the rest of India. Once caught into competition between India (majority Hindu) and Pakistan (majority Muslim) while steering itself through a difficult political landscape, Bangladesh experienced its birth pang with military coups. Then the military generals shred off their skins and formed parties and instituted democracies in order to perpetuate their hold to power in the name of the rule of the people. Constitutions were drafted to fit into their scheme of authoritarian rule. Islam was made to be an important issue in this "democratic" competition.

Apart from the parties formed by military generals, a party founded by an Islamic Mullah had played central roles in the development of democracy in Bangladesh. This party of the Mullah became the bearer of nationalism for Bangladesh. However, he was secularist, and had a leaning towards socialist ideas, akin to the political elites of India. He inspired movements which led to the victory of the party in the first ever election in Pakistan, which finally resulted in the independence of East Pakistan and creation of Bangladesh. The leader of the war of independence, Mujibur Rahman, who was charged by Pakistan as a conspirator supported by India, formed a secular democracy in Bangladesh, before he was murdered by the military. After that the country was made an Islamic state.

Since then Bangladeshi democracy had been a politics of religion, military turning civilians, family feuds between Mujib`s daughter and general Zia`s widow, and bankers and businessmen who enjoyed advantages during rule of one, or the other woman ruling as the prime minister.

This is the story of democracy in south- Asia. It is even grim when it comes to south-east Asia.

THAILAND

In Thailand the society has been ruled by kings, military men and bureaucrats (king`s men) in the recent history. After the military coup in 1932, when the absolute monarchy was replaced by a constitutional monarchy, Thailand has been plagued with coups and counter coups – shifting between representative and authoritarian rules. In this unstable political landscape all political parties have been founded and led by generals, businessmen or bureaucrats. Political power is synonymous with graft of national resources and becoming rich.

The involvement of the US in its political development had been substantial. As a strategy to contain the rise of any socialist or communist movement, in the face of the Indochina war, US support for the military dictatorship had shaped much of the Thai politics in modern time. The activities of the leftist forces in Cambodia, and Laos had left the governance of Thailand in the hands of the Generals until the rise in 2001 the richest businessman of Thailand to power.

The parties competing in Thai elections have mostly been formed by military Generals or royalist high-raking officials. The other parties have been formed by rich businessmen like Taksin, or media Moghuls. The main charges of one party against the other have been corruption, human rights violations, abuse of power in making money and corruption facilitating the growth of one`s own business empire… etc. Democracy has become a competition of the military, businessmen and bureaucrats to gain access, and take advantage and grab over a covetous free market of consumption in the name of the people.

REPUBLIC OF KOREA

In South Korea the history of democracy has started after a series of military dictatorship after the Korean War, when the US hegemony over South Korea was established. At the end of the Korean war it was ruled by a Harvard and Princeton educated Korean who converted to Christianity and had a strong ties with the US. He was then replaced by military generals..This military rules made room for a civilian presidency. The first civilian president won the election by merging his party with two other parties - one formed by a ruthless military general, and other by the Chief of the Central Intelligence. It became the Grand National Party.

Only in the turn of the millennium South Korea has seen some sunshine in its democracy, when Kim Dae-Jung came to power and instituted the values of human rights and peaceful unification with North Korea. He was a peasant son, who became an entrepreneur and took charge of a shipping company. He was succeeded by an human right activist from the same party, which Kim Dae-Jung had founded.
The opening up of the grips by military men, made it possible for the business men to become more active in politics. Human right activists professing democracies lost their ground. The CEO of the big industrial giant Daewoo became the president as a candidate of the Grand National Party. He has been newly succeeded by the daughter of General Chung (former president) belonging to the same party, which ruled before Kim Dae-Jung.

South Korean democracy has become an arena of constant splitting, renaming and grouping following regional and economic opportunities and manoeuvring towards power.

USA

The most powerful democracy today, which makes and breaks democracies in the world, is of course the US. Since the second world war, it has suppressed people's participation in other countries where there had been fears of leftist sympathies. They had hampered the emergence of democracies by supporting dictatorial military regimes, who will serve the capitalist interests instead. On the other hand, where the leftist forces had succeeded in forming governments, the US had run covert operations and intelligence activities to bring downfall of those regimes and supported political parties and groups sympathetic to the American policy. In such cases they had actively engaged in the work of establishing "democracies". The issues of human rights had come to the forefront as a strategy to raise public opinion against the leftist regimes, who, in turn, needed to suppress the capitalistic market freedom to counteract the US policy of subversion.

The birth of the United States of America had occurred through violent history of wars and conflicts for several centuries since the British, French and Dutch colonialist landed in the continent. The colonial powers, after winning lands from the natives, started warring with each other. After the natives were subjugated, and states were formed under the control of the white men, treatises were made and elections were introduced to select people to govern. Only white men possessing landed properties and wealth could vote at that time. These men became rich and powerful and did not want to submit themselves to the rule of the colonial British monarchy anymore. Through war with the British Empire they finally won independence. The commander of the war of independence, George Washington became the first president of the country. At that time only 6% of the population had any right to vote. In 1856 voting rights were given to all white men (citizens). Women had to wait till 1920 to get this right. The Republican Party won its base among the whites living in the North, who were mostly protestants, businessmen, small business owners, professionals, and factory workers. It became pro-business, supporting banks, and the gold-standard, and building of railroads and increased tariffs to protect industrial workers and industry. They became the bearer of the industrialization in the United States and the opponents of the plantation owners running their business with slave labour.

The northern industrialists and bankers rose to break the power of the southern plantation owners and wanted to abolish slavery. It gave rise to the civil war which cost 30% of men`s life in the south. From the time of the civil war to early 1930s the Republicans had dominated the political power. It came to an end with the economic crash, which created unemployment, recession and shut down of industries and closures of banks and enormous misery for the industrial workers. It was followed by the Second World War. In this difficult time a man from a very wealthy New York family (wealth from real estate and tea and opium trade with China) was elected as the president, who belonged to Democratic Party.

The situations after world war and economic crisis had a great impact in the change of policies of the Democrats. It brought the programs like social security, heavier tax for the wealthy, controls over banks and public utilities and relief for the unemployment in the political agenda. After the Second World War the voting rights were granted to the Native Indians and people with Asian ancestry. The voting rights for the African-Americans in essence remained hemmed due to requirement of paying voting tax, pass a literacy test and various forms of intimidation. After Civil rights movement of 1960s the participation of the African-Americans in the democracy has been made possible. With the increased participations of people of Hispanic and Asian origin together with the mobilization of the black votes, Democrats have surged and since 1976 have managed to win presidential campaign for half of the times. Issues like the welfare for the poor, abortion rights for the women and climate change due to the pollution of the environments have started influencing the democratic future of the United States.

However this democracy is run by patronage extensively financed by political machines and media networks while any contributions to the success of the supported party needs to be paid back by rewards.

This democracy holds the rods over everybody's head and decides where there should be democracy or military dictatorship in the world. They represent the military and economic super-power and reserve the right to make or break democracies anywhere in the world in order to stabilize the present world-order.

The ideas of democracy in the US were imported from the European soil. The ideas of liberty, equality and fraternity were by-products of the rising ambition of the French bourgeoisie to throw the old French nobility from their hegemony over economic and political power. The enlightenment philosopher Rousseau, who inspired the French Revolution, came from Switzerland, the country where democracy has functioned longest in recent history.

SWITZERLAND

Switzerland is known for its system of direct democracy, where people vote directly about matters of their concern in the municipality level. The main reason for the growth of direct democracy, where people possessing property and wealth were entitled to directly decide over the affairs of the community, was its geographical position surrounded by mighty powers at war with each other, attempting to expand their territories. Being in the middle of this turbulent region the Swiss peasantry had to arm and organize themselves under an oligarch to defend their local interests. Due to the armed nature of the peasantry the oligarchs could not turn oppressive and had to take into consideration the opinion of the local people, whose support was essential for the defence of the community against outside attack. This direct democracy was already in practice in the 13th century. The pillar of this direct democracy was the conservative peasant society, much influenced by interests of protection and supported by the conservative religious clergies.

After the French revolution and the rise of the bankers, industrial entrepreneurs and the liberal educated class, this old form of direct democracy came under attack. Napoleon made changes to bring this conservative society to unite under a parliament. There was a civil war between the old peasantry allied with conservative Catholics on one side and the businessmen, bankers and entrepreneurs, allied with the Protestants, who desired to break the culture of direct democracy on the other side.

After many ups and downs on both sides, Switzerland still maintains a system of direct democracy running down to the municipality level.

The people can challenge laws adopted in the parliament, or constitutional changes by referendum and thus keep the power of the government under check.

It is basically a highly conservative social mobilization where parochial interests of the local municipalities and cantons can be preserved and entertained and one has the possibilities to maintain age old discriminatory practices against foreigners and groups who fail to integrate fully with the local culture and practices. Until 1973 suffrage were restricted to Swiss male citizens only. All men (Swiss citizens) received voting rights in 1848.

Furthermore, Swiss democracy is highly restrictive for foreigners to gain Swiss nationalities. Only after 12 years of residence in Switzerland they may apply for citizenship, which is then put to referendum in the municipality where the person lives. After considering how the person may fit into the municipality the citizenship may or may not be granted. Here discriminations, depending on the country of origin of the person applying for citizenship, seems abundant.

While the nature of democracy in a country lying at the centre of Europe, which has rejected any integration with European Union has a shiny but extremely deceptive character, another country, which has kept itself outside integration with the European Union, Norway shows a remarkably different democracy from the rest of the world.

NORWAY

Norway was a poor country inhabited by fierce Vikings who went in plundering tours in England, Ireland, France and Russia and terrified all. They occupied Ireland, England, and northern France and established the Russian Kingdom among others. Then came the black-death which wiped out two-third of a small population of the Norwegian Vikings. After that in 14th century Norway went into a union with Denmark. The Union with Denmark lasted until the defeat of Napoleon. As a price for supporting Napoleon, Denmark lost Norway to Sweden, who was on the side of England in the war. This war seeded the formation of Norway as a state in 1814.

Before joining Sweden, a constitution was written for Norway as a state. It was formed in the presence of prince of Denmark, and military men, clergies and a few from the bourgeoisie. It was a strategy of Denmark to keep Norway in its fold. The first political parties were formed by mostly lawyers. The party supporting parliamentarian was formed in 1884. It was mostly a party of rural big peasants and city radicals. Other party was the Conservative Party, who stood against the labour movements and supported the financial and industrial interests.

Norway became independent from Sweden in 1905. By that time all men were given the rights to vote (1898). The women received full suffrage in 1913. As Norway was mostly a society of peasants and workers, in the absence of any substantial number of the bourgeoisie, the Labour Party, which was founded in 1887, came to take a central stage in politics. This party came to dominate the Norwegian politics since the financial crisis in 1930s. They believed in socialism and joined the communists in Russia. The leaders rose from marginalized working people. The faction, who took distance from the Soviet Communism and took to the policy of Social Democracy, became the main force in politics of Norway. They swayed over the political landscape of Norway before the oil boom began.

The oil boom changed the character of Norway from 1960s. The workers lost their leadership in the party and the bourgeoisie representing financial and industrial interests became more aggressive in politics. With the increased prosperity of Norway there was a flux of foreign workers. With it working class of Norway became apprehensive of the newcomers, who threatened their monopoly over the labour market. While the Labor Party welcomed labour immigration to cope with the economic boom, a party of anti-immigration, emphasizing on the ethnic Norwegian identity, became a big political force since 1970s.

Together with the traditional conservatives this anti-immigration party has become a challenge for the social-democrats and its allies to remain in domination as it had done in the past. It has also given rise to the sentiment of religious hatred and antagonism against other cultures. To counteract this development the socialist front is trying to paint the picture of Norway with a multicultural rainbow color. Thus the democracy in Norway is undergoing a tension in a period of transition that followed a reversal of economic fortune: From being a poor nation from where a large part of the population once emigrated to the US in search of an economic fortune, it has become one of the richest nation of the world where people would like to emigrate in order to find a better economic life.

The democracy in Norway is still considered as one of the exemplary democracies in the world today.

What do we learn from these examples?

Democracies take very different shapes according to the history and the cultural, political and economic set up of the country. The examples above belong to totally different historical and cultural backgrounds - from a country once ruled by the Romans, like Switzerland on one side, to Confucian culture of the Koreans.

They include the country in the centre of Europe, where the enlightenment philosophers like Rousseau and Voltaire inspired the French Revolution, and the oldest practice (after Athens in Greece in antiquity) of democracy exists, to the democracies of newborn state like Bangladesh, where religious views of Islam reminiscent of the Middle Ages, play an active role in shaping the democracy. The examples include the country, which is among the richest in the world to the country belonging to the poorest nations on Earth. They also encompass the largest democracy (India), the most powerful democracy (the US) and the best democracy (Norway), as well as the failure of democracy (Thailand).

Chapter 4
HUMAN RIGHTS
AND POLITICS

Deficiencies of Democracy Today

Democracy does not prescribe what is the most desirable social interactions and what knowledge and skill may be necessary for building a harmonious society. Depending on the experiences, knowledge, belief and awareness of the individuals there would be an intractable list of ideas and views. To take consideration of all these would lead to utter chaos. So, modern democracies try to work through a method of representation. In this prescription individual or groups of individuals coalesce around some ideas and views about the society they want to build. Different individuals or groups with different ideas and views may form different parties. Rest of the population is invited to subscribe to one or other of these ideas. Those ideas, which manage to win the sympathies of the majority of the populace, are entrusted with the task of building the social-political edifice. It does not matter if the ideas come from intelligent and wise, or deaf and blind. As long as there exists a numerical superiority it becomes the grand reason for building a future for all - whatever those ideas may be!

The belief that the most natural ideas and views will emerge from people through competitions among different ideas represented by different parties, have inspired many to adopt democratic system of governance. Once these ideas are furthermore constrained by the Declarations of the Human Rights adopted by the UN, so that no ideas that violate the principle of human rights can be entertained by any group, the democratic system can produce results which may undo the evil of history, which has created differences, divisions and disparities among human beings.

Democracy, which implies civil rights to vote and elect people to govern the society, without any restrictions based on race, gender, belief, ideas and views, has become the demand of the western countries as inalienable right of individual freedom. However, freedom needs a context in which it may receive a meaning. The context is often framed by the conditions in which one competes to survive and seeks to secure life, property, opportunities of self-realization etc.. More insecure the human life is, more restricted the arena of freedom becomes. Only in conditions where human life experiences greater securities, freedom to choose and realize oneself receives greater meaning. Freedom for a man in hunger is first to satiate his/her need for food. In exchange of food he/she will submit the other dimensions of freedom to others.

After the insecurities of food, shelter and heath are overcome, human beings seek freedom to explore the possibilities hidden within themselves as creative beings. This freedom extends beyond biological necessities to realms of the mind where one dreams, and strives to realize new possibilities of living. Only in a social order, which succeeds in freeing man from the basic needs, one can create ground for freedom where creative spirit of man may emerge. Creativity evolves according to the cultural environment where one lives, and the way the society inspires people by providing information and knowledge, and freedom to explore new frontiers of intellectual and emotional life, which are necessary for self-realization opening a new dimension of freedom. Once this higher freedom is guaranteed by a society by creating cultural environments, where new ideas can be brought forth, old views can be challenged and a climate of openness and respect for all ideas and beliefs can be ensured, the role of the human beings in building a social order becomes more meaningful.

In societies that are based on inflexible ideology, or fundamentalist religious beliefs, or cultural prejudices and superiority of one group over the others, and where people may be coerced to follow the premises of freedom imposed by dogmatic rulers, the meaning of freedom will lie in breaking away from confinement.

Only in a social order, where human beings are free from the basic needs, and liberated from the cultural dogmas and prejudices, and enjoy opportunities of engaging in the pursuit of higher freedom, which may open richer dimensions of life, human beings are able to descry the next realm of freedom representing the higher stage of evolution of society. This expanded freedom will bring transcendence of the human life through the emergence of a higher form of consciousness, which may open the doors to explore beyond the limited understanding of life by using the knowledge and methods available to man. This is a way to move beyond the world of material bondage and enter into a union with all that exist in the cosmos. The first step of realizing this freedom is the compassion, and respect and love for all. In realizing one's oneness and connectedness with all beings, who exist as wonders of the universe, the life may move forward to reach an enlightened stage of evolution. It is like moving out of darkness to light that opens the vision of existence, not ascertainable by knowledge and reason alone. This consciousness is the source of true peace and harmony in the world.

The way the development of human society is still bound in its primitive stage while hunger is not eradicated and the basic needs for survival are lacking for a large part of humanity, it is a long way to go.

Democracy is in a doldrums except in few societies belonging to the advance economies of the world. Even in these societies, narrow parochial views about the superiority of their own cultures over the other are symptomatic. Holding on to the ground of economic and military superiority they preach values of human rights and democracy to the rest of the world. In turn, to maintain this superiority they make alliances with nations where democracy and human rights may be in a dire state. They support dictators or democracies according to their own strategic necessities. When it is necessary to get supply of resources of other nations, or they need access to military bases, which may be beneficial for their economic and military dominance, they change allegiance to democracy or dictatorship as opportunistic means. Except in very few countries, like for example, the Nordics, the preaching of democracy and human rights have become hypocritical means to find ways to control the political rivals. The capitalists use it to fervently counteract the advancement of socialism and communism in countries where they have military or economic interests.

The instruments of human rights and democracy developed by the UN as Declarations of Civil and Political Rights, and Declaration of the Cultural Social and Economic Rights are the only mechanisms which inspire the Civil Society today to engage in spreading information and building awareness about democracy and human rights in the world. These Declarations are results of a political tug-of-war between the capitalist and the socialist camps. So the elements of these Declarations are an amalgamation of individual rights where capitalist interests are preserved, and the rights of the people where the collective rights of the poor and the disadvantaged are guarded against capitalistic exploitations. They are highly politically motivated and used by both camps as means to furthering their political influences in the world.

The Declarations build a ground for all people and cultures to claim their rights equally with all others and inspire minority culture to engage in a political battle to free them from the hegemony of the majority. On one hand it stimulates the growth of the political rights of the minority which, instead of forging understanding and harmony among different conflicting groups, tend to splinter the cohesion necessary to build a society of peaceful coexistence. Similarly the Declarations also provide the contrary view and profess the rights of the people and nations before the narrow interests and cultures of minorities. They argue that by this way one may guarantee the security to people as a whole. It, in turn, can be abused as means to wipe out traditions and cultures of the minorities and encroach on their resources in an undemocratic manner.

By declaring all human beings are free and equal in a world, while freedom does not exist for the majority of mankind (in the way explained), and equality is only a statement of utopian nature, which has no resonance in real life for more than 99% of mankind (except in Scandinavian), the UN builds on the ideas of freedom which have little substance in reality. By declaring the civil liberties, without any moral guidance to follow, and professing rights of all cultures and people to practice their traditions and beliefs in the way they wish, the international community promotes the problems and challenges mentioned above. It does not provide any guidance and project any vision of how to resolve conflicts and forge harmony among individuals, nations and cultures. It does not profess the necessity of higher evolution of man, and point to any particular path of building an enlightened world. By declaring that all religions, beliefs, traditions and practices enjoy the same rights to develop without giving any warning about the misgivings which they may produce, the UN declarations appear to open a stage for competitions that will generate more chaos than bring peace.

Mechanism for Realizing The Fulfilment of Human Rights

The UN adopted two Declarations on Human Rights: One on the civil and political rights and the other on the economic, social and cultural rights. The first emphasized on the rights of participation of all in a democratic process without discrimination due to gender, race and culture. It also set the premises for securing human rights and democracy by stimulating activities of the civil society, who may inform, build awareness and ensure transparencies against discrimination and abuse of power. The other Declaration focused on the rights of development of the people gaining fair access to knowledge, technology and share in the global market. It emphasized the needs for development for the people who are unprivileged. The communists and the socialists emphasized the importance of the rights to development of the people, while the capitalist nations stressed on the rights of the individuals. These Declarations accommodated legal provisions for both sides to proceed with their political and economic agenda.

Though many nations are parties to these Declarations, the real situation of human rights in the world is alarming. Mainly the developed capitalist nations are the champions in promoting the civil and political rights and democracy. They are the main donors and financial contributors to the UN. A part of these developmental aids are channeled in building the Civil Society in different parts of the world, whose main tasks are to promote and safeguard human rights and democracy. By tying developmental aid to human rights the donor countries seek to influence the development of democratic societies according to their own prescriptions. Through co-operation and dialogue they try to influence the development where the civil and political rights can be guaranteed.

Socialist and communist governments as well some developing countries, where authoritarian rule is entrenched, argue that interference in the name of human rights should be avoided. They stress on the principle of sovereignty of nations and noninterference by other countries in matters of economic or political development.

Situation of Human Rights and Democracy in the World

The poor nations have not yet been able to come up on their feet to assert themselves in a meaningful way in the world stage which is still dominated by a handful of countries. Many underdeveloped and developing nations are suffering from violations of human rights and lack of democracy.

Democratic participation of the population in the political process is mostly realized in the countries enjoying advanced economies. The rule of law and respect for human rights have grown solid roots in these places. With a few exceptions the rest of the world is reeling from violations of human rights under the grip of authoritarian rules. Most of the Islamic world is infected with military dictatorship, or authoritarian regimes. Whatever democratic process may exist in these countries are mired by violations of human rights and coerced by violence and corrupt judicial practices. In Asia, some of the previous colonies have started adopting the democratic rule and moving away from a history of dictatorship. However, in many cases, they represent nothing more than a formal democracy, where electoral process is corrupted by different means in conflict with the aspirations of free and fair participations of the people. Vote buying and other methods of frauds are known. India is the best example of democracy in the developing world. Indian democracy is mobilized by the force of poverty and illiteracy based on issues like castes, regional language, ethnic and cultural differences, religion, popularity of sport and media stars, and economic problems among others. People do not participate in voting with any greater understanding and vision beyond one`s own security for survival in a poverty stricken society. Corruption, lack of transparency in bureaucracy and police, and shoddy legislative apparatus making the legal system questionable in defending the human rights, make Indian democracy more a show of voting rights, than any meaningful participation of people in building a social order that can secure disadvantaged population against injustice and abuse of power. In this biggest democracy the historical bondage to the feudal system still plays an important role in electing its leaders. However, in spite of many loopholes and deficiencies, the rise of the activities of the NGOs and media, not controlled by the government, is making Indian democracy as an example for the developing world.

Among the advanced economies, the countries, who did not participate in colonizing the world, and where the ideas of equality had strong appeal from the past, social-democracy had taken deep roots. These countries, with a long history of social-democracy have become the citadels of human rights. Presence of well- organized civil societies, lack of corruption and preservation of high transparencies in legal, cultural, economic and political systems have made them the best example of democracy today. Other advanced nations, where colonialism have a long history, democracies carry the shadows of the past. In capitalist countries democracy is a free competition based on the strength of money, power of mobilizing the interest groups who can best support the growth of free liberal market.

Human rights are based on the idea of individual freedom and the rights to maximize one`s wealth by utilizing capital and human resources of the world. They seek to maintain economic and military hegemony over other nations. These nations support democracy, or authoritarian rule depending on what best fit their military and economic interests. When they wish to replace existing authoritarian rulers by persons of their own choice they take leadership in promoting human rights and democracy.

In communist countries, like Russia and China, the democracy is counterproductive to the goal of ensuring the rights of development of the people instead of the individuals. External actors interested in resources of other countries, play substantial roles in shaping the political development. Countries enjoying military and financial hegemony, utilize covert means to influence and manipulate these political processes. They exploit the climate of religious infighting, tribal conflicts, minority grievances, and antagonism between socialist and capitalist world views.

Human Rights and Politics

The ideas of democracy and the human rights of the individuals have become a weapon of propaganda against socialism and communism, who wish to succeed in their goals by curbing individual freedom. However, the attempts to promote democracy and human rights have generated a plethora of other forces. Those groups of the population, whose interests were once suppressed by the dominating classes, have got voices to demand their rights without feeling fear of prosecution. The competitions between the two camps have unleashed the genii who cannot be controlled anymore by traditional methods of manipulation and coercion. In nations with diverse ethnicity and cultural diversification, the battles for rights are splintering nations into groups subscribing to ethnicity and cultural idiosyncrasies. With it, political parties subscribing to the idea of strengthening local cultures, languages and traditions have started emerging by counteracting the ideas of development based on universalism. By adopting cultural narrow-mindedness and submitting to counter-revolutionary agenda, parties and organizations are divided in line with caste, clan, religious affiliation etc.. Thus democracy has harnessed an era in history, where competitions among diverse ideas – promoted either by the most ignorant, or the most en-lightened ones- are recognized as the way to achieve freedom.

The developments of technology of communication across the globe, and increased independence of the people disseminating informa-tion to the population, have added new dimensions to this process. Increased assertiveness of the journalists and reporters, and easy methods of communications in bringing information quickly to the mass are making all political systems accountable to people. The bat-tle between the two camps has extended in this arena of information and communication technology too. Advertisement, misinformation and technological warfare that may weaken others` abilities to engage the population in seeking information, have become a new method of winning political grounds.

In the historical phase, where unimaginable amount of information can be brought to people for scrutiny and judgment, mankind in every corner of Earth is being bombarded by waves of propaganda com-ing from different groups trying to catch attention and win support. Treachery, lie, false information, deceit are abundant in all camps in fulfilling ambitions of achieving success by using the mass media. The grab of power over media and communication has become an essential strategy behind social-political dynamics in achieving success in this communication age. Thus history is undergoing stress and tensions of newer dimensions due to rapid technological development and spread of knowledge and information to larger and larger mass across na-tional boundaries. It is opening up new frontiers of social and politi-cal behaviour beyond those once decided by the traditional actors like military, clergies and bourgeoisie. The entrance of the socialists and communists in the scene has helped in dismantling the walls which once kept minorities in the societies in confinement without any voice and freedom. It has become a more challenging arena to operate for all the actors. All have to take guard against violation of human rights and need to be aware of the public eyes and ears scrutinizing their behaviours.

The power of the public has strengthened with the proliferations of non-governmental organizations keeping vigilance against violation of human rights and seeking to ensure transparency in the society. They keep eyes on corruption of the ruling class with a purpose to ensure a healthy growth of democracy and rule of law. The nature of growth and efficacies of the Civil Society has become an indicator of the social progress.

Though humanity has progressed with the establishment of the supra-national body which seeks to secure peace and promote human rights, while the non-governmental organizations have proliferated with the ambition of keeping vigilance on the realization of human rights, democracy and peace the world is till bleeding in injustice and violence. In spite of the development of effective communication and information, which seek to make the actors in the society accountable to the public opinion, and the increased role of the intellectuals and humanists in moulding the social and political developments, the old mechanism of exploitation characterizing the colonial time is still holding its clutch.

Chapter 5
AGE OF INTERNET AND HUMANITARIAN INTERVENTION

The world in the 21st Century has changed radically from the days when the industrialization started. However, one thing has not changed: It is the disparity between rich and the poor inside nations and lack of parity of power between the advanced countries and the nations where economic development is still reminiscent of old time. In advanced nations people have freed themselves from basic needs like food, shelter, health care and education, as well as have access to knowledge of science, and latest developments in technologies. The knowledge of science and technology have freed them from the fear of Heaven and helped them to take destiny in their own hands through newer innovations which can change the reality and environment emerging from passive acceptance of nature. In contrast, majority of human beings in developing and less developed nations, are still duped in religious faiths and the belief in other world and believe that these invisible realms control the destiny of life. Many find consolation in the belief that a better life may follow after death, if they abide by the teachings of their religious leaders.

While women and men of the advanced nations, freed from fears of Heaven, enjoy the luxury of travelling around the world, enjoying the services and comforts which money can buy from the less fortunate ones, the majority of the humanity live wretched life filled with challenges of earning their daily breads. They live by selling products and services to be used by the fortunate people on Earth. While the rich enjoy health care of extremely sophisticated nature that includes gene manipulation and medical solutions to correct genome defects, the majority of the population in the world cannot even afford to visit a doctor who may treat the most common diseases, which need simple treatments. While the markets of the rich nations are filled with fruits, vegetables and beverages from all over the world, the people in the poorer nations cannot even afford to consume the agricultural products they grow themselves. The inequalities among the people of the rich and poor nations are absurdly high. Similar is the case within a poor nation: A handful of people, collaborating with the free global market dominated by the rich consumers of the world, may enjoy a fabulous wealth and luxuries while the majority live in a "hell" of abject poverty and distress.

The thing common between the rich and the poor nations is the fact that the economics of both sides are integrated with a global economy. The economic health of one nation is tangled in the growth and development of economics in other nations. In this global market the core-nations (advanced economics) enjoy the products and services created by the developing nations, while advanced nations control the flow of money and technology across the world. By using economic hegemony they keep the world-order intact and build economic theories, models and ideas, suitable for their goals.

The other common development among nations is the rise of the technocratic class, who are experts of economy, business and trade. A common man without expertise in global market and knowledge of the economic theories and models used in speculating about the future development of the world, and possibility of success in the monetary game, would have no clue to orient oneself in this new global-order. In such a world, the poor and the illiterates are victims of a great exploitation perpetuated by the more intelligent and smart technocrats and business-giants.

A new development in the global economy is the emergence of the technocrats and financial investors, who are forming a group across different ethnic backgrounds, nations and culture. Unlike the earlier world economic power, clustered around ethnic groups (like Anglo-Saxon for example) and belonging to a particular heritage, the new power constellation is being formed without such traditional linkage. With it the development of the multinationals and their monopoly over the future of mankind, is on the rise.

Among other important new developments belong the rise of the modern communication technology, which has opened up global networking among people across the national, cultural, economic and political barriers. Through social networking people from one corner of the world can connect with people at any other corner using internet and exchange views, likings, disliking and opinions about anything they wish to comment about. The rise of this platform is mainly contributing to juvenile fun, delinquency and moral decadence without any control of family, or authority. It is being promoted as the platform of freedom of expression and the rights to promote one self and right to defame anyone else without fearing any form of correction or punishment.

The most serious aspect of this development is its ability to agitate the young generation by feeding information (or misinformation) detrimental to social-political stability. It is being newly used as a method of spreading protests and discontents against regimes, which fall at ill-eye of the powerful nations, who can abuse the technological platform as they want. Recently the revolution of "Arab Spring" has shown its potential strength in disrupting the most authoritarian regimes and spreading political chaos in the Middle East.

This social networking is also becoming the platform of advertisement of consumer products. The big business communities make use of the personal information, left by the people in social networking sites, in order to target the potential age-group, cultural-group, or economic-groups etc. who may be susceptible to purchasing products one may produce. With the membership in social networking approaching a billion, the technology of communication is spreading its evil grip to keep human beings captive of the invisible power of the market-giants. It is also being used in attacking other cultures, beliefs and faiths, and thus strengthening the ground of a decadent culture supported by the modern communication age. The young generations, who master this technology best, are being manipulated to dismantle premises of cultures which may contradict with the juvenile spirit of delinquency and chaos of unguided will to be free.

In the face of this development, the traditional religion is facing a crisis. While in the advanced economics the faith in religion is dwindling fast, and being replaced more and more by the values pivoted around money and success in the market, the mass, in the developing countries, are experiencing the pain of transition from age-old faith to modern consumer life-style. Now the modern super-markets are becoming the main attractions to visit than the temples and museums exhibiting historical objects, or promoting spiritual dimensions of life. Thus human beings are being uprooted from the ground on which human civilization had found security, solace and comfort for several millenniums. Not only people are losing connections with history, they are being bombarded with information about products, entertainments and self-help to find happiness and freedom by using one's unguided free will. As most people do not have capacity to absorb the information flow to develop a sound perspective of life, they are making themselves captives of the lower nature of man.

In this atmosphere, the slogan behind freedom is "democracy and human rights". In the international politics democracy and human rights have become the instruments to check any development of socialist, communist or authoritarian rule, which may threaten the free-market philosophy, and curb the authorities of the technocratic elites and their compatriots in the military and the business world. The demand for good governance which may foster democracy and human rights are becoming ways to interfere and militarily intervene in the sovereignty of other nations.

This new dynamics of changing the unwanted rulers and replacing them with people more open to free-market and fuller integration of the global economy, which is more and more controlled by monopoly-capitalists and multinationals, is taking the name of "humanitarian intervention". Not for love for life, but for securing a stable economy, dependent on energy-resources and raw-materials, the western democracies have set the process of democratization in the world (except those places in the Middle East, where authoritarian rulers are allied with the market and helping to stabilize the supply of oil to the Western hemisphere).

Of course, not everything is so bad: The movement of democracy and human rights have some side effects which are freeing women and minorities (in particular) from traditional oppressions practiced in many societies. It has generated movements where the poor and the middle class have got opportunities to voice their opinions in issues of immediate importance to them in the local communities. It has brought a rising tide of participations in securing the interests of groups, who had remained outside the game of power, since the start of history of modern civilization.

The aspect of social changes, brought by democracy and human rights, are mostly affecting the societies where women and minorities lead most undignified life. Especially it is the case in countries where the ideas of the fundamentalist Islam still have strong appeal. The idea of liberating the women from their traditional roles is seen as an affront on their religious beliefs and social stability. The free-market philosophy, grounded on a banking system, which is based on interests and profits, is also another point of divergence from the Western culture, which ignites hatred against the Western powers. This hatred is compounded with the historical rivalries between Islamic civilization and the culture of the West based on the Christian heritage.

Heading Towards a Disaster?

The biggest tension in the world today is caused by desire of the western powers to maintain their economic and military dominance of the world as they had done in the colonial time. The survival of the Western economics and the geopolitical dominance over Earth's raw-material and labour depend on the vital supply of oil from the Middle East. Control of the oil fields by the West would increase their advantage over countries like India, China and other Asian economies, whose rising economic strength may threaten the western superiority. So the West needs to keep the energy resources of the world at their disposal and control. This energy issue, in turn, brings the West in conflict with Islam because of the rivalries of the different Islamic groups with each other.

This conflict is becoming quite dangerous. The western countries need to trade carefully in the minefield of the Middle East where different fundamentalist Islamic groups fight with each other for establishing Islamic values and practices following Koran, which are in contradiction with the market oriented values of democracy and life style preached by the western culture.

The central spot of this danger lies in the region around Israel, who is equipped with modern arsenals to keep its supremacy over the Islamic nations who, in turn, would like to annihilate Israel (only if they could). Israel is an ally of the superpower leading the Western economy and military strength. So the hate of Israel can only simmer in words, and not in actions. Any action will be tantamount to bringing upon doom on the countries in the region.

The politics of the Middle-East is full of contradictions: The Islamic culture on one hand is in conflict with Western values and culture; on the other hand the West is the protector of political stability in the region marred by religious rivalries among different Islamic groups. The poverty in the region is also a fertile ground for growing faiths in religions. The societies, which have seen little reform in modern time, and remained stagnant in superstitious beliefs and practices, which are in disharmony with the idea of democracy and human rights, are pulling the world towards violence and terror.

The most effective way for the West to operate in this region has been the strategy to utilize the conflicts among different Islamic groups so that the power to control oil resources may not go out of hand. Depending on the given situation they support one group, or the other, without any other purpose than to seek dominance over the vital energy supply. If necessary, they ally with the most fundamentalist group, violating the most basic of the human rights, in order to keep the enemies of Western dominance, in check. Some claim that the west has contributed to the rise of the terrorist organization like Al-Qaida, whom the West fears most these days. Even today they finance and give military trainings to the enemies of the states, who are not willing to serve the interests of the West.

Governed by the economic interests and filled with the ambition of maintaining hegemony over other nations (as they had done in the past) the West follow the strategy of utilizing antagonism among religious groups to secure their goal. This treacherous policy, though successful, has not gained any respect for the Western values. The confrontation between Islam and the Western culture is getting worse due to such political manoeuvres.

However, the dissatisfied groups have little means to challenge the Western economic and military superiority. Therefore, they choose the path of terrorism. By killing themselves in suicide bombing with a hope to weaken the enemies, the terrorists are, in a desperate way trying to assert their power over the super modern weaponry, supported by the highest technological innovations of time. It may seem pathetic. But, it keeps the Western power alert and vigilant about their securities under terrorist threats.

The newest introduction to counteract terrorist activities is the invention of "drones", which can search, find and strike targets with sophisticated weapons with the help of robots. These unmanned military crafts are becoming the most effective equipment to combat the growth of terrorism in Afghanistan and Pakistan these days. Thus while on one side the West is killing the terrorists, and at the same time financing rebel activities against "undesired" state by supporting the terrorists (as in Syria), the West is moving along a dangerous path.

The nations, ambitious of getting out of the grip of the western dominance, are exploiting this situation by siding with the opponents of the groups allied with the West. Recently the conflicts in the Middle East around Syria and Iran have divided the members of the Security Council into two groups: On one side US, UK and France, and on the other side China and Russia. The West would like to intervene militarily in Syria and Iran on the pretext of democracy and human rights and peace and security in the region, while the Chinese and Russians, after the military intervention of NATO in Libya, have fully understood what may lie behind the Western cry of democracy and human rights in Syria and Iran. NATO has sent patriot missiles in Turkey, neighbouring Syria and Iran, while the Russians have equipped Syria with sophisticated ballistic missiles, which may evade the Patriot surveillance.

While the conflicts related to Syria and Iran still remains highly inflammable and dangerous the West has these days got embroiled into an even more dangerous conflict at the door step of Europe. This is also to do with the issue of energy supply to the western economy. A large part of the gas is delivered by Russia to Europe through pipelines passing through Ukraine. Russia wants to maintain its control over the Caspian oil and gas, while the West wishes to access it without Russia controlling the flow. So in the name of democracy and human rights, the West has supported uprising in Ukraine in order to oust the Ukrainian president who had favoured relations with Russia over the European Union.

It has created a dangerous situation: Russia has responded by annexing the naval base of Crimea and destabilizing South East Ukraine in order to foil the western plan to put the government of their choice in Ukraine. The conflict between NATO and Russia is getting worse by everyday.

With the rising economic owe in the West, and the increasing economic power of China and Asia, when two former socialist/communist countries have joined hands with Russia against the Western hegemony, the world seems to be entering into another phase of history. With globalization, the disparities between rich and poor are increasing. More the west is being exposed about what they have done in history, and what they are doing now, the cultural clash between Islam and the Western culture, in particular, is becoming more and more intense. More and more science and technology is dismantling the edifices of religious beliefs, more and more the young generation in the West is losing illusion about the meaning of life and getting drowned in a chaos of information,which pushes them into a consumer culture without meaning. More the Western culture is being transmitted through social networking and media entertainments to disrupt the traditional societies, which have not been exposed to the good side of the western cultural heritage, more the young generation in the developed countries are falling into an abyss of a cultural vacuum. Neither they are able to identify themselves with their own traditional heritage, nor can they absorb what are good in the Western society. This generation floating in the "vacuum" is an easy prey of the modern consumer culture, which is overwhelming all and emerging as the globalized evil. More the issues of democracy and human rights are being abused in order to tear down traditional patterns and change cultural practices, traditional societies are becoming disillusioned about the meaning of democracy and human rights.

Economic crisis, cultural clash, terrorism and the market culture, transforming the urban areas in Asia as a "big bazaars", are more and more increasing the risks of a global disorder. With it the young generation all over the world is being imprisoned inside a bubble of "nothing" created from "nothing", which is expanding fast inside a "vacuum" of a valueless world floating without directions at this moment of history in a free-market.

In this situation the world is warming up as the result of fuel consumption needed to sustain this economic development in the world. The global warming is becoming an issue of great concern, threatening the future of mankind. Many argue that the consequences can be catastrophic both politically and economically. Experts are forecasting that the changed weather pattern of Earth will bring with it more flood, cyclones and droughts disrupting the agricultural production while creating inundation of valuable fertile lands in some places, or lack of water needed for irrigation in other areas. The feared rise of the sea-level in the near future, as the results of melting of ice capped on the poles, may push population in hundreds of millions from coastal areas, creating economic refugees who may contribute in creating political turmoil. Scarcity of food supply compounded with the migration of population to new areas brings omens of potential danger and catastrophe on Earth. Seen in the perspective of the conflicts, already raging on Earth, the future of Earth is full of serious warnings.

Challenges of Peace

At the present moment even the most progressive societies are undergoing stress in fulfilling their democratic and humanitarian aspiration. The influx of the immigrants in Europe, who wish to adhere to their religious belief and continue to practice the culture of the society from where they have come, is the main cause of this social tension. At the same time the deteriorating socio-political structures in many developing countries, governed by authoritarian rulers and afflicted by the problems of poverty, are forcing population to move to affluent part of the world. The struggle between the undemocratic fundamentalist religious rulers and the democratic progressive society is becoming a conflict between technologically organized superior nations with people who wish to assert themselves by adopting the means of terror. While one side clings to religious belief and values of old traditional cultures, contradictory to universal human rights and democracy, the other side builds mechanisms in the global arena to bring an end to fundamentalism which tries to subjugate others by acts of terror.

This increased tension in containing the religious fundamentalism, combined with the conflicts between capitalist and communist ideologies, is building a polarized world, where promotion of democracy and human rights is considered by the opponents, as a tactic of the capitalists and old colonial powers to interfere into the sovereignty of other nations. For example, operation of NATO in Libya in removing Colonel Gadhafi from power has been interpreted by Russia and China as a way of the western powers to maintain control of the energy resources they need for their economic development. According to their view by inciting demonstrations and public protest in demand of human rights and freedom, similar tactic is underway to remove Assad from Syria and bring Iran with its oil reserves into their fold.

Thus human rights and democracy has many facades. While country like Norway, who enjoys sufficient oil reserve, and is not to any major way affected by immigrations of religious fundamentalists, promotes human rights and democracy from humanitarian point of view without carrying hidden political agenda, US exploits democracy and human rights as a way of interfering into sovereignty of other nations in pursuit of economic resources and military bases.

The US, enjoying the position of the uncontested superpower, rattles saber in order to bring changes in the world in whatever way they may want. When it is possible to act by building consensus in the framework of the UN, the US works in that way. If they fail to gather support in the UN they go in their own way by building alliance with nations friendly to them, and/or rely on the military firepower of NATO.

The success of maintaining dominance in the world depends on the technological military superiority as well as hegemony over the global financial market. It, in fact, reflects the same psychology which has driven human beings to subjugate and dominate others for ages.
Thus the nature of ruling the world is a mixture of old tactics of making alliances, or breaking alliances according to one`s need to execute programs which will bring success, without concern for what may be universally considered as right or wrong. The emphasis is more on the security through building alliances with others, who have similar cultural history and values. The antagonism against other values, and scepticism about other cultures, hinder humanity to find a common universal ground on which one may build a peaceful world. Unless the moral foundation, on which different cultures and nations draw their

nourishments, converge, the prospect of peace will remain far-fetched.

The United Nations

The United Nations was created after the Second World War to tackle the challenges of the problems of the survival of mankind together. After its inception, the main challenge became the issue of nuclear catastrophe. The five nations, possessing nuclear capabilities at that time, were given the responsibility to develop mechanisms to bring peace and security on Earth. They constituted the Permanent Members of the Security Council. The other nations joined the organization to seek a platform to interact with other nations and build their own security of survival.

The organization became an organ of reconstruction and development of the nations deprived of the opportunities of growth because of the lack of financial resources, technological backwardness and lack of good governance. The developments of nations, which provided the citizens with the security of life, were considered essential for maintaining peace. The UN became as organ of developmental aids and a platform for negotiations between the rich North and the poor South. The US became the main aid giving nation. It also provided the main funding for the running of the organization. After the Western European nations, after Second World War, economically came on their feet and reinvigorated their economies with the help of the US, they also started contributing to the development projects in the poorer countries – mostly in Asia and Africa. The development assistance became a way of maintaining power of influence in the old colonies, and thus finding opportunities of market and investment in other nations. In some cases the development aid was linked with the opportunities to establish military bases.

These days' humanitarian interactions to protect people from violations of human rights are becoming more and more an open issue to debate in the international forum. The first of such intervention sanctioned by the Security Council was conducted by NATO in Yugoslavia in order to stop ethnic cleansing. It was possible as consequence of demise of the Soviet Union and political reorientations of the countries of the Eastern Europe. More recent intervention occurred in Libya, where mass agitation started against the rule of Muhammad Gadhafi, as a part of the "revolution" in the Arab world, which was triggered and sustained by social networking. The brutal reprisal that followed in order to quell the agitation brought charges of crime against humanity against Gadhafi and paved the path of military intervention by NATO (Security Council was more reserved at that time in sanctioning a full military intervention). As Russia and China accepted the idea of establishing no-fly zone over Libya, it gave NATO the pretext for intervention.

Syria is another country where the "Arab Spring" has bloomed and fights between Sunni and Shia have begun. President of Syria, Assad has mobilized its military power to quell the opposition financed and trained by the West and its Arab friends in the Middle East. US, UK and France have tried to get sanctions from the Security Council for a military intervention in order to replace Assad with a "democratic" ruler. This time China and Russia have blocked all efforts of such a military move. The Western powers have now moved behind the rebels trying to throw Assad, while Russia and China still do not budge from their position of supporting the Syrian regime.

In this situation, the military intervention by NATO in Syria and Iran without releasing another World War seems remote. These developments are converging to a dangerous moment of confrontation between the Western countries, Japan and South Korea on one side, and China, Russia, Iran, Syria (and, may be India) on the other side. History will witness who will come out victorious in this geopolitical battle for the future. Whoever becomes the winner, the world will usher in a new age for mankind. The new war will have much deeper impact in changing the history of mankind than any other events in history so far.

What will be the nature of the new world? What will be the new elements in the social order that will emerge after the demise of the modern age, which started with industrialization? As said before, nothing is written in Heaven. The new world will emerge from within us, by using the power of the human mind, which beckons us to create a new civilization. We must look deeper into our mind, and gaze at the events of history, which has brought us here, in order to understand our own nature and the possibilities of our evolution as a "higher-man".

Chapter 6
WHAT NEED TO BE CHANGED AND CHALLENGES AHEAD

Before delving with the question what specific changes we may need in the present world-order and social-political culture, which the globalization is spreading across the world, we need to understand the basic aspirations of the human beings, whose fulfilment may make life happy and secure. Among others they include the following

- The security for survival by winning over the needs for food and shelter for oneself and the family;
- The knowledge about the world and the surrounding environment which may make life less harsh and easier to live;
- Get possibilities to explore the world and experience freedom to seek development of the mental and physical abilities one may possess;
- Receive rights over the resources of mother nature equitably with others and the opportunities to feel that earth is a free playground for all;
- Find cultural arenas to share feelings and emotions with other fellow human beings, which may give expression of the spiritual and artistic nature of the human mind;

•The desire to be loved, and to love and feel comforts and joys in the company of others;

•Enjoy trust of others and psychological security in relationships;

•Feel harmony and peace with oneself and the world around;

•Enjoy freedom of speech, belief and faith, rights of association with others and opportunities to participate in activities of the community.

What may win loyalty of the people?

Most people will be loyal to any social-political order, which may fulfil the above needs of life. The political governance, which protects the rights and creates conditions that can provide the fulfilment of the harmonic and peaceful life, while respecting freedom of the individuals without jeopardizing the freedom of others, would be the desired form which draws loyalties and support. People expect decrees and rules, which should be applicable equally without discrimination that may bring justice to the society. The violation of these decrees and rules may cause the society to slide into chaos. The people also wish to reserve the rights to change the rulers, who may fail to deliver a social-political order which can keep peace and harmony in the society. Once the rulers deviate from the rule of law, which should be equally applicable to all, and favour a few, or a particular group in order to strengthen the hands of power which can be abusive, the system turns authoritarian.

To find the rules and decrees that may deliver justice to all has been the main problem to deal with any social-political structure. Human beings are often prone to errors and faults. In the Chinese civilization the rules and decrees were seen to correspond with the Heavenly way. Once the ruling of the mortal world fell out of harmony with the Heaven's way, the chaos and disorder were supposed to descend on the society. The Emperor was seen as the representative of Heaven and celestial harmony. Like the Chinese, most other civilizations have also alluded to Heaven as the source of laws and decrees. The emperors and kings have represented the Heavenly will. In the name of Heaven people have been made to accept the ruling systems. Even these days, the deprived population of Earth relies on the belief in Heaven as the source of justice and hope for life.

However, Heaven fell with the rise of science and spread of knowledge in the industrial age. With it the mortals, who did not have the rights to represent Heaven but became economically powerful to challenge the old order, formed groups who competed for gaining loyalties of the population. It opened up the history of development of democracy in the world. The democracy became the way to attract supporters for different views and ideas to deal with the social-political issues, which could satisfy the needs of different groups comprising the mass.

From Heaven to the hands of the mortals

Democracy became a way of different interest groups to compete with each other in drawing support of people who had a mixture of different levels of education, views and economic strengths. Instead of the monopoly of Heaven, shared by the monarchs and clergies, now the bankers, traders, businessmen and the feudal lords all formed their groups to take part in the process of sharing of power and decide over the rule of law which should form the new social-political order. The material interests of property and wealth, and to secure the economic and political strength of the group to which one belonged became decisive factors in this competition. Different parties were formed, who participated in the democratic aspirations of people seeking to share power: Besides the party supported by feudal lords, religious party, socialist party, communist party, capitalist party, fascist party etc. mushroomed before and after the Second World War. Instead of decrees of Heaven the constitutions, under which the democratic competitions could be conducted, were written by mortal men. Though freedom, equality and justice were mentioned in these constitutions, the democratic competitions became ways of instituting injustice. The loopholes provided by the existing inequalities among diverse groups of population, combined by lack of education and freedom of the vast majority of the mass aggravated the state of justice instead. The population, who had been exploited by the feudal class and kept ignorant for centuries, with a fear of Heaven hanging over them, became targets of the parties, who wished to win their loyalties in order to come to power. Exploiting fear, ignorance and lack of understanding of history by the unenlightened mass, different parties, rallying under the umbrellas of different ideologies- varying from religious fundamentalism and capitalism to atheism and socialism- offered promises of fulfilling the needs of life. However, with this democratic process the inequalities increased, the freedom of the elites of the society multiplied at the expense of the servitude and misery of the poor. What turned as justice for the economically and politically powerful became injustice for those who lived hand to mouth. The poor and the disadvantaged remained outside the protection of law and enjoyment of security of life. However, democracy could run its show because the loyalties of the poor and the ignorant mass could be purchased by the economically powerful ones during the days of election.

The democratic competitions stimulate many different means to attract voters: The use of media, including newspapers and television, is the most effective means to get the programs of the parties to the people. Advertisement and billboards are other ways to catch attention and propagate messages. Democracy is based on the free choice of the people to support one set of political program over the others, which one may consider more potent in bringing changes to the society that will fulfill the desired needs of life. Often the media stars including film stars and famous sportsmen are brought into this political advertisement campaign to make election more attractive, whose perspectives about values are mostly confined to what they watch on the TV screens. Those parties who can show faces of the popular stars may win supporters more easily. However, to do this one needs financial or political strength to own, or influence, or manipulate the media shaping much of the democratic process. In countries where poverty and illiteracy is a major issue, the votes can be purchased by the candidates willing to win power. Some moneyed citizens use democracy as financial investment. The amount they invest in buying votes open up possibilities of much greater return through corruption and abuse of government power once one gets elected.

In most democracies, the financial abilities of parties to advertise, and make use of the media in the democratic campaigns, as well as the level of education and awareness of the people about the rights and responsibilities of choice, decide the outcome of elections. In societies where the awareness about the mechanisms by which democracies can be manipulated by money and abuse of power elites is low, the election functions as a roulette of money, advertisement, propaganda and low-grade entertainment appealing to the instinct-bound man. In many situations, instead of emboldening the values which could help to build a harmonious and peaceful society, where everybody may enjoy equality, freedom and dignity, democracy brings forth the nature of selfishness and greed instead.

Rule of money and market

One essential aspect of democracy these days is its relevance in injecting economic growth by stimulating the development of the consumer market. Democracy goes hands in hands with capital investments and imports and exports without trade restrictions. It is becoming more and more capital driven political culture. In countries where the political system is restrictive to the capitalistic mode of economy, the power of the capital is turning decisive in removing the hindrances by using the mechanisms of the global financial systems, on which most nations are more and more dependent for their economic success. The increased economic globalization is making the political systems more streamlined according to the principles of capitalism. The influence of the big powers, ruling over the global finance, is becoming more and more apparent through the economic development of countries being governed more and more by the financial technocrats. The external forces are shaping the democracies of the world by capital control and different economic measures. The local political actors often find the alliance with the external powers as opportunities to remain in power by democratic means. Without such democracy, the rulers lose legitimacy and may face financial pressures from the global actors. Even the military autocrats are being forced to change their clothes and wear the democratic outfits in order to be accepted as legitimate actors in the global market system.

Democracy turned into demonocracy

The ideas of democracy were meant to introduce a political process which may guarantee freedom, equality, and justice in the society. The ideas of the enlightened philosophy were supposed to fulfil the needs of the people to find security, peace and harmony with nature.

Instead of making the world safer the democracy seems to have become a harbinger of danger and catastrophe. In opposition to creating a social system where all may enjoy security of life and guarantee of fulfilment of the basic needs, the democracy has increased the freedom of a few, who are equipped with economic strength, to exploit insecurity and needs of the less fortunate ones. In the western supported democracies the emphasis is given on greed of the individuals who may wish to amass power and wealth by using the existing disparity in the world. It is epitomized by the idea of the individual freedom to freely engage in pursuits of making money and associating with interests which may bring monopoly of power in a few hands. In these democracies the legal systems also function as means of justice for those who can pay the high charges for the lawyers to settle disputes with their opponents. In many legal dealings supports of money and political power play significant roles.

The focus on the capitalist ideology, driving the process of democracies, have made consumer culture the foundation of values in the modern society. In this democratic culture everything is getting monetized: Everybody is free to snatch opportunities, according to their abilities, in utilizing means to make one`s fortune in a free market arena, where people with political and financial muscles can always exploit those who possess little or no other means but to sell their labor and toil. The winners of such a democracy are those interest groups, who wish to take advantage of the freedom and strength of the groups, which make the world more unequal, and sow seeds of divisions among people of different cultural background, belief and faith. Apart from the countries where the ideas of social-democracy have roots, the democracy has become a platform of expression of intolerance and discriminations against minorities and weaker part of the population.

In short, democracy has become a way to maintain hegemony of the market power and transform values of life into monetary units, where happiness is judged by the consumer power which one may possess. This has become a method for the capitalists to perpetuate the dominance of its ideology and control of the population of the globe through a process called globalization which is giving rise to more and more monopoly. Thus the laws and rules created by the mortals have taken away from the human beings the dimensions of life that may give meaning, love, harmony and sense of belonging to the nature.

In this democratic doldrums education is also oriented to provide knowledge which will help the market and industry to function better. There is more and more rush for management studies, banking and finance, and technologies that have greater market values. In this knowledge rush, the truth is often depicted as the one which are promoted by those who possess more military and economic prowess. With it the superiority of the culture of the West are being pushed on the global arena, which In turn is destroying the old values which once contributed to the social harmony in the past in many countries. Market power is creating a universal consumer culture, which has more appeal to the nature of man bound to instincts.

Finally this development, based on the consumer culture, is creating impacts on the environment by releasing more and more pollution in nature. If the weather pattern has changed, as results of the economic activities, as reported by the UN, the freedom to consume, ensured by the market, is going to bring catastrophic consequences on the life of a large part of the population of Earth.

Thus in many ways the democracy is fulfilling the reverse of what should make life harmonious with nature. In modern democracies, instead of the higher nature in man, the demonic instincts seem to be taking over the control over the society.

Challenges ahead

In a globalized world where the consumer culture is gaining more and more supporters, while a vast mass of unprivileged and uniformed population constitutes the labor pool, on which the consumer market relies for its existence, what would be ways to bring change, which may fulfil the aspirations of life which are mentioned in the beginning of this chapter?

The global market is being carefully protected under surveillance of the capitalists, who make use of the intelligence apparatuses, supported by advance technology, to follow the behaviour of people across the globe. Thus developments of organizations and ideas, who may rise to challenge this existing world-order, are kept under watch. On the other side the digital communication age is being used as the portal to expand the market to the private space of life of the consumers. The social networking sites are becoming windows to advertise products and services to the account holders who now have surpassed more than a billion in number in both Facebook and Twitter.

These days the most natural mode of social interactions by direct contacts, are being replaced by interactions through the virtual cyberspace, which is open to listening and wiretapping by the authorities who control the communication technology. Market is spreading its shadowy nets everywhere, while swapping trust and security among individuals by suspicion and anxiety of a menacing power which threatens human freedom in a disguised way. The people are being alienated from each other. The users of the social networks often operate by hiding their real identities in order to spread ideas and views which threaten to destroy trust, respect and understanding among each other. From Fascists, Nazis and religious fundamentalists to military dictators and intelligence networks of the democracies of the world all have set their networks to take advantage of the freedom of flight of the citizens to express opinions and views through the web and mobile handheld units.

Beside these cyberspace actors, there exist different institutions which support the social-political structure. They are mostly run by financial supports by the states, or by the money sponsored by big business or wealthy persons. The institutions receiving money from the big business are often captive of the interests of the market. The state run institutions are mostly reflections of the historical past and bearer of activities which promote national interest, glory and power. The major arbiters of the state are the financial institutions, industrialists and the military. They often collude together to decide the nature of the democracy and freedom the citizens may enjoy. The news media often act as the mouthpiece of the state policies for propaganda in shaping public opinion. Those political parties who win the support of these groups may count on success.

Outside these institutional structures, there exists in different degrees the presence of civil-society in different countries. Many of the civil-society organizations involve themselves with the questions of the governance, democracy and human rights. However, these organizations existing in the developing countries depend on the assistance from western nations for their existence, and naturally are susceptible to the policies of the donors. These organizations may be utilized for covert political activities to bring change of people in the government, who are desired by the donor country. In this way, through the human rights activities too, the market driven forces take control of the course of the political future of the democratic nations.

Is there any alternative?

One may sink in despair and like to argue that the historical conditions is the prime mover of the human civilization and so there is nothing much to do in practice in trying to change the state of affairs. However, we should reject this understanding of civilization which accepts circumstances destined by the forces which have controlled history so far. Instead one needs to understand that the history is a product of the human will and conflicts of interests among groups possessing different states of evolutions of the mind. So far, the lower nature of man has come out as triumphant in history by accumulating power and wealth in a few hands. The innovations and creativity have been directed towards dominance of one over the other, and abused in the form of inventing military technology in support of the instincts of preying on others and securing one's hegemony.

One needs to understand history as a ground that takes shape according to the will and actions of human beings. It reflects no other laws of nature (or mind) beyond what evolution of human consciousness may reflect. As it will be explained in the context of the enlightened world in a later chapter, the human consciousness has many levels - from the lowest level, inspiring animal instincts of the predator and prey, to the highest form where man may identify oneself as a part of the cosmic mind, who is one with all. In this higher level, love and compassion and the consciousness of unity of all existence become the bearer of the will, and provide initiatives for taking actions which may shape a new social-political order.

Leaving man to his/her lower nature will create a civilization which we have witnessed in the past and witnessing now. We need to dismantle the structures which we have built on such primitive ground, and usher in a history of the "higher-man", instead. It needs a total transformation of awareness and knowledge of man of himself or herself, and the vision of the possibilities of human kind to ascend to a higher-stage. With this knowledge, vision and awareness one must build a new framework of history. This implies a vision of "revolution" and the beginning of a new civilization.

Elements of history, which have kept human kind a prisoner of the animal instincts, must be replaced by higher-values and awareness of the possibilities of our life as bearers of a great mind animating the universe. Man is the maker of his/her own history. No fictitious force other than man's will is the foundation of its path of evolution and growth.

In a world, which is infected by so many malaises, how should we create a foundation and structure of such an "Enlightened World"?

First we need to have a clear concepts about the nature of an enlightened system and how it may differ from the economic-political systems which have existed in the past? We should understand how to overcome the obstacles which have hindered human civilization so far in finding ways of happiness and meaning of life beyond personal greed and private interests. Is there any moral rule written in Heaven, which should guide us to formulate model of social-economic behaviour?

So far, most rules have been created by human beings based on their understanding of the world, history and themselves. In the past the religious teachings and scriptures have been used to find allies of power among the fellow human beings and Heaven has been exploited in order to ascend to power and maintain dominance over the ignorant mass.

These days this story has changed from allegiance to Heaven to Free-Market force. More Heaven is falling, more the knowledge of science and technology are replacing views about cosmos, nature and our own mind. With this development, more and more Free-Market values are determining the premises of happiness and joy of life. As a consequence human being are getting disoriented in the world and loosing direction to live and act in ways which may bring meaning to living.

In this circumstance, the laws and regulations of the modern democracies are being written by mortal women and men in defence of ideas which may be appealing to the voters. These democratic social-orders are run by people, who wish to amass political and economic strength by rallying people behind their ideas wrapped around some party political ideologies. In this democratic competition voters can be bought with money, or manipulated by offering more purchasing power which brings consumer happiness. However, there exists no direction, goal or vision beyond keeping momentum of economic growth supporting the ever growing consumer-culture and captivating people in the activities related to the Market.

In order to steer the civilization towards the vision of the "higher-man", we must know who we are, where we are, and why we are? What roles can we play on this cosmic stage? What should be our destination of life in this amazing universe?

So, we need to conceive our position and relations with the rest of the creation first. We must have answers to the questions posed above. The way we see ourselves, and understand the meaning of our existence in the cosmos will decide our path.

The belief in the old ideas about the universe and ourselves, where things happened according to the decree of Heaven, has weakened. Instead, scientific knowledge has gained prominence in the world of the modern man. However, one should not delude oneself to believe that what we know as scientific truth is the final answer about the universe and ourselves. They could be erroneous and may require revision.

The views about the nature of creation of the universe, and the reality, on which the ideas of the enlightened-world are based in this book, are fundamentally different from the views about universe and life, which are propagated by the main stream media and the institutions today. We need a change of paradigm before we may usher in an enlightened civilization on Earth.

The knowledge about the new universe and nature of the reality entangled in multiple spheres of consciousness will be the foundation on which we may build this new-civilization. Knowledge of the profound nature of ourselves and the universe will be source of values and visions to guide us along the enlightened-way.

In the next part of the book I shall focus on ideas of this enlightened democracy. In some sense it resembles the idea of Heaven's Way by the Chinese.

Chapter 7
SOURCES OF VALUES: UNDERSTANDING OF THE UNIVERSE AND OURSELVES

We Live in a Designed Universe

In an entangled micro and macro-cosmos every existence has a role to play in sustaining the existence of the whole while maintaining a design of the universe which reappears in similar way from the largest to the smallest structures. Inputs from large to small and feedback from small to large uphold the wonder of existence, which represents a harmony and order beyond comprehension of the human mind. The universe plays a cosmic symphony, where from the tinniest to the largest structures all are tuned to play in synchronization to create the orchestra eternally being staged everywhere in all scales in an incredible perfection. Although every note being played is impermanent and returns again and again creating infinite variations in time, the musical melody being played through new births, evolutions and decays remain eternally the same. Universe annihilates and discards actions and motions not falling in harmony with the whole. The entanglements in different scales create an appearance of complexity beyond the power of visualization by the human mind. It arranges beauty and order from any chaos which may appear due to accidental events falling out of the unity and perfection of the design.

Evolution of life towards higher stages of consciousness

In this universe the foundation of life is rooted in the physical world. It rises as a phenomenon arising in the process of organization of the physical world at a very high level of complexity. Such complex organization finds ways to exist and take part in the entangled world, where every existence is dependent on everything else, by developing codes of behaviour fitting into the design of the whole. Higher and more complex the codes, it emerges as a form of consciousness, which represents a new level of reality transcending the physical world driven by laws. It takes the form of a supra-material world. A form of "will" develops which conducts and guides the life process. Higher the organizational complexity and more extended is the arena of interactions with the world, the form of consciousness gets elevated to higher level. Once the physical environment remains conducive to the existence of higher existence, life seeks to organize itself towards higher form through a process of evolution. The higher life generates more in the conditions of order and harmony existing in the environment. Similarly, existence of higher life contributes to the development of new environments of greater order and harmony. Primitive life forms are less capable of affecting and bringing changes to the environment, which decides the premise of their existence. But higher life forms can reshape the environment and create conditions of its growth and development by using their will and choices. In this way life ascends in the level of consciousness from a stage of pure defensive strategies of survival to a creative level of reconstructing its own destiny of survival by using will, intelligence and choice. Thus life is no more molded by natural conditions and the law-bound world alone. The emergence of creativity in higher form of life sets a stage of experiencing new-dimension of reality, where it becomes an arena which can affect life and at the same time can be affected and changed by the presence of life.

The human beings have attained an even higher form of consciousness than the stage of creativity by which one can imagine and project new conditions of reality outside the existing frame, in which life may be bound. Not only the human beings can construct and shape a new environment of survival of its own choice by using creative means, and overcome the blind dictates of the natural world, they are able to gaze deeper into the mind to find the best possible choices. Imaginative creativity can produce many suggestions which may not be sustainable against possible changes in the environments and conditions in long or short term. Projecting the consequences in the future and recapitulating the past experiences and making logical judgments and analysis on the basis of the experiences and knowledge human beings demonstrate even higher power of the mind. To construct an understanding of the nature of reality and life and build a consistent picture about the nature of existence and cosmos, based on some logical and rational principles, is another aspect of this higher-mind. With it man can reveal the working principles of nature and gaze deeper into the mystery of existence. By entering this realm of consciousness one may understand the unity of the micro- and macro-cosmos and gain perspective about life in the entangled universe.

However, the logic and reasoning, with which one gazes at the world have roots in the relations existing in time and space and events which follow from causal connectivity. Our brain has the capacity to relate to experiences not bound in time and space. These experiences appear as bizarre phenomenon which cannot be explained by logic and reason and are often known as spiritual experiences of something existing outside the perceived world. It constitutes another dimension of human consciousness. In this level man may experiences unity of the living and the nonliving worlds emerging from a realm outside space and time, which constitutes the highest state our consciousness.

Several Spheres of Consciousness Forming Our Will

Primitive man

Before understanding enlightenment one needs to understand how our brain works, the consciousness arises, and we connect ourselves to the rest of the living and nonliving world. The primitive brain is the site of the life forces which decide the strategy of survival and defense. Hunger, thirst, fear, apprehension of danger, sleep, rest, need for reproduction for continuation of the species etc. are common in the animal kingdom. They arise as automated biological response to the need for nutrition, and demand for adjustments with the environment where one's existence may be endangered due to competitions with other animals, similarly trying to secure ground for survival by preying on others. Brain must remain constantly alert about the possible threats and the potential benefits in adopting particular strategies to defend itself in a given circumstance. This information are processed in our primitive brain which creates the consciousness about the nature of the reality colored by hunger, thirst, fear, competition, reproductive urges, instincts etc. Unless the threats are removed, and life is secured for physical survival and reproduction of the specie the consciousness remains grounded in this primitive state.

Imaginative and creative man

In environments, where the basic needs are secured and threats to life from competitors are minimized, the brain can activate other modes of consciousness beyond the primitive instincts. For example, it can use its capacity of dreaming. By fetching information about the reality experienced before, and setting elements of experiences in an imaginary context one may construct an imaginary "reality" of one's own choice and desire, which has not existed before, or may never exist in reality in the future. When this process occurs under the supervision of an awakened mind, which scrutinize and analyzes the imaginary events, and able to foresee the consequences of such interactions of events in the context of the real life, the mind is heightened to act in a higher plane. Dependent in higher skill of imagination, once the imaginary events are acted in the real world, they do not conflict with the working principles of the reality. Instead, they may help man to transgress the boundaries imposed by the reality. Thus the world, once appearing as imagination, becomes an integral part of a new reality. The ideas projected by the mind can then partake in the movement of the world, which becomes a new stage of life. This is how one may step into a higher level of consciousness. By using the power of intelligence and the capacity of dreaming and desiring, one transgresses constraints of the primitive mind and becomes a creative being. However, the power of one`s capacity of dreaming, desiring and making use of the intelligence are rooted in the cultural environment and the framework of knowledge about the world available to individuals in the cultural arena which they share with others. More rich is the environment, which gives access to the deeper understanding of the nature and its relations to us, more equipped a human being becomes in establishing himself/herself as a creative individual.

Scientific and contemplative man

However, the creative man may live in many levels of consciousness depending on the framework of knowledge, and the desire and vision, which drive him/her. More the desire and vision of a man are constrained by self-interest, or norms and prejudices of a particular culture the lesser becomes the development of the creative mind. More the power of creativity is based on knowledge common to the larger part of humanity, and free from the prejudices of the cultures, where man may find oneself, greater becomes the realm of the creative consciousness. Scientific knowledge, which is universally valid across all cultures, provides an expanded foundation to achieve a higher consciousness. Deeper the knowledge, the richer becomes the vision of unity of all life, and our original source in the same elements as we find in the stars. A truly scientific man develops a consciousness, which embraces the activities of the brain entangled with the dynamics stirring the cosmos. By using the power of the prefrontal cortex, which helps us to focus our mind and contemplate deeply about the nature of things, one can unravel the relationships existing in nature. With it one may gain a higher level of consciousness. Through logical introspection and reason one may achieve a vision of the world existing beyond the realm of our crude perception. By entering the domain of pure thoughts one may experience a transcendental sphere which can be known through mathematical relations.

Spiritual man

Brain itself is the source of the spiritual experiences which manifests as bizarre phenomenon incompatible with information processed by the parietal lobe. It has been observed that artificial activation of the temporal lobe can bring forth such spiritual experiences. The so-called spiritual nature is thus embedded in the mechanism of the brain. It is there to direct the mind to explore outside the realm of the sensory perceptions, and the spheres of logic and reason. It is our brain's way to lead us from the human state of consciousness to a superhuman consciousness which defies the boundaries of time and space. It opens a channel to explore the relationships which lie deeper than the reality bound in space-time dimensions we are used to. It is a higher form of consciousness because it can guide the evolution of the brain towards a newer height where all living and nonliving beings appear as one. In this sphere the micro-cosmos and the macro-cosmos merge as the same arena of a cosmic consciousness. Man may not be able to unveil the mystery of its nature by the logical methods of understanding because logical reasoning is rooted in the experiences of events occurring in space and time. One may question its objectivity and it is precisely what one should object to from the point of view of reason: It indicates the limitations of objectivity as defined by our still evolving brain and consciousness rising thereof!

View about God

The question of the existence of God arises in human consciousness as a pointer to the realm which may exist outside time and space. It is difficult to form an understanding of God, because it cannot be described by knowledge and logical constructs of the mind. God appears as an experience mediated through the brain, which connects man to the realm outside the world of perception and knowledge. God represents the highest state of consciousness which can affect the mental world of man by impinging on the mind as a force that can alter human state of consciousness. Thus it can open doors of experiences outside the world bound in time and space, though indescribable by language and reason. Varied ideas and images of God appear due to different ways the one experiencing it may project the indescribable experiences on the "screen" of the phenomenal world. The nature of God takes shape following the knowledge and the capacity of imagination and creativity of the one who describes the supernatural realm. God may appear in mind as a state of consciousness experienced by the mind but can never be known by using knowledge of the world known to man. When one describes God, it is delusional like a reflection of an invisible realm in the visible world. However, it exists as the experience of the highest state of consciousness pervading the cosmos which can penetrate the physical and mental boundaries of human existence.

Meaning, Freedom And Good And Evil

Meaning

The idea of the meaning is defined according to the stage consciousness, which the person, who is asking the question has achieved. For many, meaning lies in an achievement towards fulfilling a goal. In the primitive level, meaning is measured by output, which is beneficial to the question of survival and meeting the instinctual needs. In the level of the creative man, meaning can be fulfilment of creative urges in freeing oneself from the dictates of the law bound world, and creating conditions which may make life easier to live with desires and visions of one's own. Here meaning lies in the freedom of realizing the self, and creating imprints of one's own mind in the reality where others may also participate. Thus meaning lies in discovering an identity as a self, seeking expression of freedom outside the realm of survival. For a scientific man meaning can be synonymous to accessing information behind the hidden marvels of nature and identifying one's ability in controlling the natural order according to one's will and desire. Here meaning lies in acting on the conditions, and controlling the forces which once subjected human life with disadvantages. It is akin to seeing oneself as a "mini god" who has triumphed over destiny. For the spiritual man meaning extends outside the joy and triumph of the "superman" in experiencing the dimensions outside the spheres of perceptions and understanding. One may ask what does one gain by striving to attain these experiences. How can man benefit from such experiences? What is the final destination of such a spiritual enlightenment?

If meaning is posed as a question of making some sort of benefit in life, which may contribute in changing the human conditions (both psychological and physical) then the spiritual man attains it by bringing forward the evolution of the brain to a newer stage. By developing the aspects emerging from the temporal lobe one brings the evolution of the brain to a newer dimension, where consciousness of the physical existence may attune itself to super-consciousness. With it one can view one's existence beyond the physical state of things as represented by perceptions and thoughts bound in space and time. It is beneficial in terms of forging an existential premise with the cosmic dynamics which is churning the consciousness arising in the brain to move forward to higher and higher stage.

Where will it end? Can anyone reach the absolute end (if there is any)?

The question of the absolute meaning does not revolve around the benefits one can derive by attaining a state, but to move as a process and be a part of the super-conscious scheme, which does not have any goal or end. Concept of end is based on our idea of time, which begins and ends. In super-consciousness there exists no temporal start or end. It emerges from itself in order to churn the whole, which is bound in the form of the cosmos. In this process it recedes within itself to bring renewal of every existence in a newer stage. It is a symphonic orchestra of incomprehensible complexity and coherence that rises while breaking apart in order to join in the process of emergence again and again. It is this movement in which all consciousness participates. Or, in other words, all consciousness emerges from this movement. By knowing its presence and experiencing its minutest manifestation in the living beings, the enlightened spiritual man can help us to rise higher than where we are. There is no final meaning but an eternal meaning, which is a process that does not have any answer to the meaning in the way we may like it to conceive with our limited power of the mind.

Meaning of freedom

Democracy, which implies rights to vote and elect people to govern the society, without any restrictions based on race, gender, belief, ideas and views, has become a universal demand by people all over the world as expressions of freedom. However, freedom needs a context in which it may receive a meaning. The context is often framed by the conditions in which one competes to survive and seeks to secure life, property, opportunities of self-realization etc. More insecure is human life, more restricted becomes the arena of freedom. Only in conditions where human life experiences greater securities, freedom to choose and realize oneself receives greater meaning. Freedom for a man in hunger is to satiate his/her need for food. In exchange of food he/she may submit the other dimensions of freedom to the society.

After the insecurities of food, shelter and heath are overcome, human beings seek freedom to explore the possibilities hidden within themselves as creative beings. This freedom extends beyond biological necessities to realms of the mind where one dreams, and strives to realize new possibilities of living. Only in a social order, which succeeds in freeing man from the basic needs, one can create ground for freedom where creative spirit of man may emerge. Creativity evolves according to the cultural environment where one lives, and the way the society inspires people by providing information and knowledge, and freedom to explore new frontiers of intellectual and emotional life, which may open a path of self-realization – a new dimension of freedom. Once this higher freedom is guaranteed by a society by creating cultural environments, where new ideas can be brought forth, old views can be challenged and a climate of openness and respect for all ideas and beliefs can be ensured, the role of the human beings in building a social order can become more meaningful. In societies that are based on inflexible ideology, or fundamentalist religious beliefs, or cultural prejudices and superiority of one group over the others, and where people may be coerced to follow the premises of freedom imposed by dogmatic rulers, the meaning of freedom lies in breaking away from these confinements.

Only in a social order, where human beings are free from the basic needs, and liberated from the cultural dogmas and prejudices, and enjoy opportunities of engaging in the pursuit of higher freedom, which may open richer dimensions of life, human beings are able to descry the next realm of freedom representing the higher stage of evolution of society. This expanded freedom will bring transcendence of the human life through the emergence of a higher form of consciousness, which may open the doors to explore beyond the limited understanding of life by using the knowledge and methods available to man. This is a way to move beyond the world of material bondage and enter into a union with all that exist in the cosmos. The first step of realizing this freedom is the compassion, and respect and love for all. In realizing one's oneness and connectedness with all beings, who exist as wonders of the universe, the life may move forward to reach an enlightened stage of evolution. It is like moving out of darkness to light that opens the vision of existence, not ascertainable by knowledge and reason alone. This consciousness is the source of true peace and harmony in the world.

Good and Evil

Good and evil arise from the existence of will that acts in the world in order to fulfil a goal and serve a purpose, which a person intends to accomplish. The definition of good and evil takes different meaning according to the perspectives from which one makes the ethical judgment. In the lowest sphere, where man behaves as an animal, the will to live and act in order to survive, reproduce and safeguard the progeny could be judged as sound ethical acts, though others may perish as results of these pursuits. Seen from a situation, where physical survival against the predators is not any longer any urgent necessity, the will to steal others of their freedom and the means of subsistence, which can create conflict and chaos in the society, can be called an evil act. The goodness may be defined as the aspect of the will which seeks to create order and harmony in a world, where others participate and strive in building a common ground of security of survival for all. The willful acts aimed to exploit physical or mental weakness and ignorance of others in order to organize and lead a social process, which promotes the advantages of a few over the majority, are contrary to the development of harmony and peace in a society. The will, which sees the power of human organization in bringing forward the higher nature of man, creates the foundation of good in the society. It brings forth order and harmony through co-operation and sharing. Those, who promote the knowledge of the enlightened world, and act with the awareness of the unity of all, and inspire others to march towards realms outside the boundaries of ignorance, and thus draw humanity towards a larger world beyond the sphere of the instincts, could be considered as the bearer of the power of "good".

Enlightenment Without Religion

What is enlightenment?

In the religious context enlightenment is considered as a spiritual revelation that can bring deep insight into the meaning and purpose of the existence of all things in the cosmos, and thus a way to arrive at the understanding of the mind of God, who is assumed to be the creator of all. It is believed that this profound spiritual understanding can be achieved when man has reached a higher level of consciousness above the mundane consciousness of being entrapped in the world through sensory perceptions. This higher consciousness is proposed as the way to understand the unity of all things and feel one with all existing beings. This heightened perception of the nature of the reality generates compassion for all living and nonliving beings. With it the mode of communication with the world change from the perception of life as a field of struggle, competition and suffering to view that considers all as the part of the Self.

Though talk about enlightenment usually appears in religious context as a spiritual path, it can also be understood in a nonreligious way as the path to understand the complexity of the existence of the living and the nonliving worlds entangled together in the cosmos and attain a full comprehension of the existential situation which is dependent on the existence of all.

Who is an enlightened man?

An enlightened person is aware of the progressive evolution of the consciousness tied between freedom and constraints existing in the environments, in which human life proceeds. By achieving enlightenment he/she may not enter into a blissful state of happiness while transcending all challenges of survival. It is a way to achieve a more comprehensive understanding of the working of the mind and brain and gain deeper insight into the nature of the consciousness and its evolution with changing circumstances of life. An enlightened person makes journeys in all realms of consciousness, without being attached to one particular sentiment by knowing the necessity of all forms of consciousness, which follows our evolution. It is bound to the state of existence, which has evolved from nonliving matter and are destined by the laws of nature as wells as the dynamics of survival and evolution of the species. An enlightened person does not distance himself/herself from the less evolved mind, and refrains from clinging to the state of the mind in search of happiness and bliss. For an enlightened mind there exists no suffering or happiness. Only an awareness of the complexity, wonder of the cosmos, in which mind is moving and taking parts in the events of things, suffuse his/her emotions. Knowing that nothing can escape the churning of the cosmos and the dynamics of life and death, by which things regenerate from the cessation of things, enlightened being does not profess cessation of the events and route of escape from the cycle of life and death. Instead, for him/her the way the cosmos works, as a wheel of life and death, is the only way through which one must grasp the meaning of life as a perpetual drama of coming and going life after life. By remaining tranquil, without being moved by the events, which the challenges of survival and evolution may bring, and remaining unperturbed by the ecstasy of happiness, which successes and achievements may tempt, the enlightened mind seeks arena of consciousness that cannot be penetrated by mundane suffering or joy. He/she knows the journey is long, and man exists in the cosmos as a bearer of the task which may bring mankind to a higher evolutionary path.

Compassion is a way to engage oneself in this process that can bring mankind from one realm of consciousness to its next stage. Knowing the circumstances of life, which may have deprived a human being of freedom from the instinct-bound state, the enlightened being seeks to change the conditions of life, which may make others free. An enlightened being brings the messages of the higher worlds to those who are bound in the primitive level while bearing compassion and love for all. When he/she enters the realm of the creative man, he teaches them how to overcome the prejudices and views, which may bind man into actions beneficial to groups, cultures and races. Instead he/she promotes the view of creating conditions of reality from which mankind may benefit universally. He/she asks the scientific man not to serve any nation or group, who may abuse knowledge and innovations to the advantage of dominating and suppressing other nations and groups. Instead he/she appeals to them to make his or her knowledge and innovation available to all in order to free mankind and thus contribute to the higher evolution of man. Enlightened man acts in love for mankind instead of serving powers which may bind others in chains.

An enlightened man is also a spiritual man in the sense that he/she does not mark the limits of knowledge only to the sphere which can be grasped and understood by scientific knowledge alone. The enlightened being is aware of the possibilities which parts of our brain may indicate. He/she knows about the evolutionary journey in which all life are embarked on. By accepting the limitations of methods bound to the perceptual world which remains in the causal bondage in time and space, he/she professes the need to heed to ourselves through the brain about the nature of the world which points to a realm beyond time and space. By listening to the inner self one can bring the journey of the evolution of mind to a higher ground where cosmos has kept open a store of wonder for us.

However, no man or woman can be enlightened in the fullest way before all mysteries of the universe are fully grasped, and one is able to realize oneself as the universe itself. Though this journey has no end, the enlightenment can be achieved in comparison to the ignorance in which man may live. One talks about Buddhahood, which is the end station of such a journey.

Such idea of Buddhahood is synonymous with the cosmos itself in all its infinite complexities, which is beyond the capacity of the brain to grasp. So an idea to attain such a state is an illusion for any existing being. Buddhists have concepts of Bodhisattvas, who are embodiment of the highest consciousness achievable in the mortal sphere.

The journey of enlightenment is a journey to achieve the state of the "higher-man", who can teach and guide the unenlightened beings about the higher paths.

Why should one seek enlightenment?

Enlightenment is a progressive process to realize one's potential as a human being. Every human being has the potential to realize oneself in greater and greater arena outside the bondage of the nature and the instincts by expanding and making use of the higher capacities of the brain. By freeing oneself from the instinct-bound level one can realize the creative potential, by which one can overcome the slavery of the forces which control the life. Thus one can create foundation of one's own life in a way which is not controlled by external forces alone. Similarly, through creative activities and power of imagination and intelligence, one can bind mankind together as a unity, and make voyages in the realms of the universal man with richer and richer shores to experience and explore. This is a sphere where through music and arts, for example, one may communicate about the invisible worlds of the mind. Those, who aspire for a higher state, can enter the cosmic arena through scientific reasoning and make a voyage into a space and time billions and billions of light years across. Those, who endeavour to explore realms beyond the confines of time and space, may explore the aspects of the temporal lobe and thus connect to one's own nature as a part of a cosmic mystery that can never be fully grasped.

By seeking such progressive enlightenment one can help the specie to which we belong, to attain a greater realization of its potential as a cosmic creature, which may help to free mankind from the vagaries of the law-bound natural world. It is a journey towards freedom of the mind and a way of experiencing heightened emotions of love and compassion for all existing beings.

Who can achieve enlightenment?

Enlightenment is an endless journey through which the brain evolves. By making use of the different parts of the brain one prepares for the journey to be made in one`s life. According to the level of knowledge. to which one is exposed, and depending on the nature of the environment in which one is constrained to live and survive, the awareness of the reality gets defined. The level of consciousness is accordingly bound to reflect the situation of which one is a victim. One`s journey begins where one is. Every human being has the possibility and potential to undo the state where one finds oneself. However, any such effort to free oneself from the slavery of the state will bring struggle and challenges. With the help of enlightened teachers one may find ways to deal with these challenges and pave one`s way to freedom. Man can progressively advance towards higher and higher stages. One, who is bound in hunger and need, must first free oneself from the bondage which creates the conditions of such suffering. It is his/her first step to freedom. With this freedom achieved, one can then build conditions of one`s own choice and desire by using creative power of the mind. Again the enlightened teachers can be the guides. Freeing oneself from dogmas, prejudices and thoughts, and following the universal man, who embraces whole of mankind with compassion and love, one should move in the path towards enlightenment. Thus the journey can proceed towards higher and higher realms with the help of the guide. Every human being has the possibility to transcend to a higher level of consciousness, which means partially freeing oneself from the conditions of bondage to the world where one may feel confined. Enlightenment is a journey and a process, not a final destination where one may arrive at and can be finally free from the challenges which every creature must face in the cosmic drama. It can be achieved as a step wise movement from one realm of consciousness to the other. No one can achieve enlightenment in its fullest sense, but everybody can make a journey towards more freedom. How far one arrives towards the goal depends on the willingness of the man making the journey to heed to the advice of the enlightened guide, and the circumstances of life in which one may remain bound.

Concluding message

Enlightenment is a journey in search of freedom from the bondage of the law-bound world in search of a greater dimension of existence that cannot be perceived by, or grasped by an unenlightened mind. In the final stage of the journey, man experiences the inner dynamics of the cosmos, which churns all existing beings and sustains the existence of the whole, which has no beginning and end. By elevating one`s mind to listen to this orchestral symphony, one experiences the power and force which bind all as the great cosmic wonder, penetrated by a cosmic mind, which can never be grasped with human language or thoughts. Being a part of this cosmic wonder one can experience life as an abode of love for all – the living and the nonliving.

So the message is: Move forward from where you are; seek freedom and strive to go beyond the conditions which bind. Know that there are greater and greater possibilities hidden within you. Listen to an enlightened guide and act to discover newer frontiers of the mind. Proceed until you hear the cosmic symphony in the inner realm of your mind, and see the frontier of the brain where consciousness merges with the realm of super-consciousness, which impregnates everything existing in the cosmos. On the way, experience the power of an enlightened life of love and compassion for all.

Chapter 8
ENLIGHTENED WORLD: FOUNDATION AND STRUCTURE

Vision of an Enlightened-Order

We need to realize that we are not animals, who live in order to exploit opportunities of competitions and gain supremacy over others in nature. We are much more than what the need for our physical survival and security may dictate. As mentioned before we are bearers of several levels of consciousness, starting from the reptilian and mammalian state of evolution of the human brain to the development of the prefrontal cortex which is the powerhouse of reason, rationality, and the temporal lobe with which spiritual unity of life with the cosmos can be understood, experienced and felt. We are manifestation of a wonder in the cosmos, which holds the enormous complexity of the living and nonliving worlds in a unity, and gives us the opportunity to experience order, perfection and beauty through our own mind. Our life is a fortunate opportunity to experience the highest level of consciousness that can emerge as our greater aspect of mind as a force of love and compassion suffusing all. Behind the physical visions of things, triggered by neurons in the brain, there exist visions in the mind in different "realities" not ascertainable by using only the animal instincts. Those invisible "realities" bring creative urges in the mind in the form of ideas, thoughts, imaginations of the higher-mind, with which one may reconstruct the sense-bound reality. By this way one may transcend the limitations imposed on us by law-bound nature and recreate a reality of one's own choice. Thus, mind becomes the foundation of creation of reality in a higher-stage. The purpose of human life is to experience those domains of "realities" which do not become visible through crude manifestations of the senses in the perceptible world. By exploring those domains and elevating the mind to experience the "higher-world", man has the opportunity to enjoy the unfathomable wonder and beauty which hide behind the apparent chaos in nature.

Vision of an enlightened world is a vision of beauty, love and wonders which can make life a paradise of happiness and joy. This vision is restive on the state of mind through which one experiences and gazes at the world. The chaos and suffering are not products of any unavoidable nature of the reality which is separate from the mind. It appears as projection of the mind in the sense-bound world. The projections depend on the knowledge of man about one's own nature, and the nature of the world in which one sees oneself bound. The man, who is bound to his /her animal instincts and has not realized the domains of possibilities that can be explored in the "invisible" realities of the mind, may see a dark and a chaotic world in realms where the higher man sees the lights of the cosmic beauty and order.

Vision of the enlightened world is the vision which emerges through knowledge, creativity and understanding of the unity of the living and nonliving world. It unveils when one is able to open the windows of greater "realities" lying deeper in the unfathomable realm of the mind. These windows can be opened by accessing knowledge, and utilizing creative urges that may stir the mind, and detaching oneself from the lower-nature of the instincts. By sinking deeper into the depth of the mind in search of beauty and wonder hidden behind all, and remaining awake about the marvellous nature of the cosmos, one may ascend towards the enlightened path.

It is a vision of an opportunity of a journey of life, in order to put in action the power of the higher-mind in shaping human civilization, which leads us to act and live. Instead of sinking into greed and competitions in order to win dominance over worldly resources, which keep the majority in the world in slavery and chain, and desiring to increase power and wealth only in a few hands, one must usher in an age of the higher-man, who will teach human beings the joy of life in love and sacrifice. It is a vision of an age of beauty, harmony and peace built by the power of the higher-mind.

What is an Enlightened World?

The envisioned enlightened world is a social-order under enlightened governance, which promotes the best possibilities of development of human beings towards the path of evolution to a "higher-man", who is equipped with knowledge, power of creativity and rational reflections and connected to inner realms of the mind, which is the source of love and compassion for all. It sets as its goal to inform human beings about their higher potential to evolve beyond the conditions where they may remain imprisoned, and equip them with necessary knowledge and opportunities of expressing creativity with which they may reshape their conditions beneficial to evolving towards the higher stage. The enlightened world is built on the power of the mind with which one may transcend towards higher level of consciousness, which can reveal the unity of life with the micro and macro-cosmos, and chart the meaningful roles which human beings may play in creating peace, harmony and beauty in the society.

Primary conditions for building an enlightened world

The most primary condition of an enlightened world is the existence of an enlightened governance, which bears the visions of the higherman, and the goal of establishing peace and security for all. The basic securities people need are the securities of life against hunger, shelter, indignity and threats to life due to disease and natural calamities. The next level of securities involve freedom to access knowledge, information and know-how with which one may improve one`s conditions of development, choose and protect one's conviction and belief, and secure one's aspirations to improve the present condition of living. After these fundamental securities are guaranteed, one requires support to see things in life from greater perspectives beyond one's individual framework of life and need, and open oneself outside one's belief, prejudices and ignorance which create hindrances to the evolution of society.

The enlightened social order hinges on the ideas which have universal acceptance by all as the most logical and reasonable platform of values, without being clamoured and compromised by the narrow interests of some people or groups. The enlightened governance makes the universal values, which may contradict and oppose the cultural beliefs and superstitions of some people, as the foundation of its policy of enforcing justice and rights. The universal values should not be derived from the culture of the dominating nations and people who may try to impose their culture on the rest. These values should be built around the views about universe, nature and life, which form the foundation of the ideas behind the enlightened world, through participation, dialogues and discussions among people of different nations and cultures. The atmosphere of war and conflict must cease before instituting the ideas of an enlightened society.

Tasks of the enlightened governance

The enlightened society should take guard against the abuses of power by people enjoying economic and military advantages, who may try to dislodge the world from fulfilling the vision of an equitable society. The enlightened governance should emphasize on the necessity to guide and inform people, who are less educated and informed about the potential of human life. By inspiring the more educated and informed population (who are also the bearer of the universal values), to participate in the activities of guiding and teaching the uninformed, the enlightened world should build the basis of a more and more enlightened society. In order to succeed, one needs to secure the atmosphere which may create openness to universal values and respect for opinions and ideas which may contribute in building a stronger platform of cooperation among different ideas. With it, one needs to take distance from any dogmatism which may contradict and oppose the universal aspiration of mankind. All religious teachings not in conformity with the universal values and aspiration of freedom and evolution of human race towards a "higher-man", must be abandoned. At the same time ideologies, which may tend to spread chaos and break social cohesions built on the values of love and compassion for all, must be checked.

Accepting the reality that most societies in the world are mixtures of heterogeneous population as regards the level of education, security and opportunities, enlightened world needs to remove disparities which cause inequalities among human beings, and strive to provide everybody with equal opportunities of development as a free human being. Any distinction made on the basis of race, gender, wealth and power must be eradicated, and all forms of manipulation exploiting the physical, mental, or economic weakness of others must be strictly prohibited. The freedom of a few dominating and controlling the others by abusing higher technological means, not available to the majority, must be brought under rule and restricted in order to guarantee freedom for all. Free competitions must be checked in a society where a few may possess every advantage of exploiting the financial, technological and material resources and others have nothing but their labour and life to sell. Society must remove all categories of differences which may resemble as class, and build a classless society pivoted on universal values of love and compassion for all.

Competitions may generate innovations and creative solution to win over the competitors. However, it becomes brutal and inhuman when innovations and creativity are used to amass fortune at the cost of misery of the less fortunate ones. The economic playground of the human should not be similar to the animals of lesser intelligence. The competitions in order to survive, as in the animal world, can be a necessity in a world suffering from scarcity of resources. In the human sphere innovations and creativity should be stimulated in order to provide means of survival of all and not as ways to possess maximum wealth and power with which one may control, manipulate and exploit the rest.

Societies should build cells of well informed and educated human beings, whose tasks would be to bring information and knowledge to the less fortunate ones and empower them with technological and other means to resolve the disparities in the society and thus establish the ground for building an enlightened generation. The cells should take guard against the failure of instituting the enlightened social order at different levels in the society, and ensure availability of justice to all.

A Way to Move Forward

What should be the way to move forward in building such an enlightened world?

An approach to accommodate all ideas, thoughts, belief and practices as equally valuable to human progress would be a naïve and an ignorant man's approach. To ascertain the right path one must have knowledge about the nature of the world and the dynamics which operate in shaping history and accordingly take steps in building a progressive society.

The particular approach in a particular place should depend on the social and historical context where one intends to bring changes. In the society, where hunger and basic needs are the most pressing problems of survival, the issue of freedom should revolve around the way human life can be secured against these needs. The most meaningful social engagement in this situation should be to bring people out of hunger and needs first before anything else. We do not need societies, which profess democracy as the power of the individual to caste vote in the ballot boxes, but do not allot resources and adopt methods to free the poor from hunger and needs. It will be misunderstanding of democracy if the rich can buy votes of the poor and manipulate the social system by exploiting illiteracy and ignorance of the insecure people. Practicing democracy while keeping the wealth and access to resources only in a few hands, and conducting a formal show of equal participation of all in a voting process, will be against the aspiration of freedom of the suffering people. They need rulers who have love and concern for their freedom.

How to establish a political order of the enlightened rulers, while the political culture throughout history has been a history of oppression and exploitation? Without curbing the greed of the wealthy and the power hungry players, and setting conditions which may empower the poor to challenge injustice and manipulation, the politics of instituting a process where all are entitled to vote, will not bring any meaningful development of freedom. One must ensure methods to empower the disadvantaged with means that can halt the ambitions of greed that has corrupted the development of humanity and hindered mankind to evolve in a higher way. The way the idea of democracy is professed by the capitalist societies, is certainly not conducive to freedom of the poor. For democracy to have any meaning in furthering freedom of man, it has to be given direction and control. It will bear a vision that individuals must understand the value of compassion and share the suffering of the others in order to ensure the security and freedom of all. An ideology of a brutal competition must be replaced by the idea of the brotherhood of man.

The way to an enlightened world is a progressive path: One needs to build it step by step. The societies, who have been able to secure all life against basic needs, and created conditions where creativity can flourish, the individuals should be stimulated to seek freedom of individual self-realization. In this level of progress of freedom, knowledge, information and openness to the outside world are great assets. In societies where individuals enjoy similar economic strengths and opportunities to access knowledge and get stimulation to realize their higher potentials, the ideas of human rights take altogether a different dimension. All ideas, which project to bring advancement and evolution of humanity, must remain open to discussion and scrutiny in a progressive society. Where this process is mired by the imposition of particular view, and sanctity of traditions bearing a particular culture, the possibility of human freedom becomes stagnant. Without creating an openness and respect for freedom to challenge ideas of human progress, the path of democracy will fail. When democracy can be manipulated by a dominating culture and belief, while seeking its superiority over other cultures and ideas, it will lose its meaning. In a true democracy that seeks to create freedom of man where individuals may contribute to the advancement of humanity, one must take distance from any fundamentalist view whether of religious or philosophical nature. Here all dialogues and discussion must pivot around the question of building an enlightened world.

Democracy should not be dragged into the quagmire where all views, ideas and cultural prejudices and superstitions may claim equal rights and clog the advancement of the society. Although one may identify oneself with a particular culture and belief, where one feels comfortable and happy because one is brought up in this environment, everybody should be taught to seek a greater perspective beyond one's own narrow parochial world. Dialogue should not mean the path of regressing back in the dark ages of history by accepting the developments which has led us to wars and conflicts in the past. The developments based on religions, and extreme views, which may threaten the security of others, should be discarded if humanity must progress and be free. Instead of letting all cultural practices and prejudices occupy the cultural stage of the world with equal status, one should generate a process of dialogue among all cultures to set up guiding rules that will help mankind to seek a path of evolutionary progress. In the name of democracy when ideas, bearing superstitions and prejudices against other culture and people, may aspire to rise to take hold of power in the society, one must win over them and strike hard to foil such evil aspirations. Instead, they should be confronted with the views and aspiration of the universal man seeking the enlightened path. However, one should not be naïve about this superior form of democracy: To institute its reign one will need courage to challenge the powers of the diverse power-hungry groups, who have dominated the history in the past.

Enlightened Democracy

Enlightened democracy is a vision based on the view that mankind needs guidance and direction to move in order to achieve social and political order which can be the foundation of peace. It sees the necessity of the world to move forward to higher and higher stages of evolution, where every human being has the responsibility to participate. It views situation of the world existing at this moment of history, where diverse stages of social evolution live together (some societies are still in a primitive stage bound to hunger and basic needs, while a few has progressed), as an unsuitable arena for growth of greater aspirations of man as creative beings, searching meaning and greater possibilities of self-realization. These aspirations can be realized only by building a foundation of enlightened democracy.

Enlightened democracy professes the view that human beings are endowed with the power to realize themselves in ways that may fulfil the meaning and purpose of human existence. Once they are equipped with knowledge of nature, better understanding of the dynamics of history, and become aware of the power of the higher consciousness, human beings have the possibility to evolve in the direction of the "higher-man". This aspiration to evolve towards the "higher-man" will be able to steer human civilization towards harmony, beauty and peace. Instead of ushering in chaos, which may arise when one tries to understand the evolution of history as a process emerging in a random way resulting from of interactions of diverse interests, enlightened democracy will fulfil the meaning of life as bearer of cosmic mind.

However, it is not something one may achieve in the same pace everywhere. The varied historical conditions will decide the starting position from where one would need to set the goal of bringing changes.

As said before, it should be viewed as a progressive path: First, one should free man from hunger and needs, and then from ignorance, prejudices and superstitions derived from tradition and belief which may bind man to a particular culture. Then one should seek to empower human beings with understanding and vision, with which they may be able to appreciate the values and ideas of the enlightened-order accepted by all people and cultures of the world. In this process they should be guided in freeing themselves from the narrow views inherited from the culture where one may have been born and brought up. It is a way to march forward by breaking away from views and practices of an ignorant world, and instead make a journey as a part of the whole of humanity moving towards a common goal by sharing same values and visions.

Enlightened democracy prescribes the values and visions that can be accepted by human beings of all nations, cultures and races once they are equipped with knowledge and information about the nature of the world, the dynamics of the social and political cultures and the inner nature of themselves as creatures possessing higher power of consciousness. It can pave meaningful paths of freedom leading to higher and higher ways. It is a path which needs to be trodden by using the power of knowledge and visions of the unity of all living beings with the cosmos, permeated by a meaning that one needs to explore. It is an exploration and journey towards higher heights of the mind towards freedom that may liberate us from bondages that the mechanical world imposes on our existence.

In this journey we may find many of our fellow human beings still struggling to free themselves from the basic needs. Enlightened way is a way to act to bring changes in the world that will create conditions of freedom for them. Beyond pursuing the path of knowledge, the enlightened democracy teaches man to be compassionate about the suffering world. Success of enlightened democracy hinges on the prerogative that societies produce teachers and guides who will transmit knowledge and vision and inform people about the direction and goal one should pursue.

With it, one needs to promote the growth of an enlightened Civil Society i.e. the community of teachers, trainers and guides, who will form the backbone of security and peace in the world.

Purpose and Goals

The beginning of the 21st Century can be characterized by a development of a system where the rich monopolizes the investment and the supply of products in the market, the middle class consumes, and the poor produce the goods with their labour. The middle class also runs most of the service sectors. With the increasing middle class the consumer market expands, and the economy, which bases on the balance between supply and demand, grows. The producers in the bottom get some benefit as a trickle-down effect, and some of them may elevate themselves into consumer class. The main benefactors of this consumer driven economy are the monopoly - capitalists, who defend democracy and human rights of the individuals. The democratization process, the way it works today, makes it easy for the monopoly capitalists to reach the largest number of consumers in a free-market system, and perpetuate the mechanism at work without generating much friction. The middle class, who never received any power in history before, finds in this system a freedom to participate in changing the economic and political dynamics of the society simply by their power of consumption, and the rights to elect those, who may sustain the power of the middle class through this new market mechanisms. Technocrats help to run this system as stooges of the monopoly-capitalist market.

The enlightened order will be totally different. Its driving force will be no class, no nation, and no group. Its leaders will be the enlightened human beings, who may belong to different classes, caste or creed. However, they will all identify themselves as the bearer of the higher nature of the human mind. They will remain at the apex of the new order.

Of course, one needs to make assumption that these enlightened human beings, who are driven by the desire to serve greater interests of mankind, beyond the narrow interests arising from the lower-nature of man, exist in all societies at all time. Though, it is clear that in modern time their role in history has diminished, and got drowned under the chaos of the market culture. The positions of these human beings, who act out of idealism and vision, and believe in the power of a society based on love and compassion, must be reinvigorated in the society so that they may help to carry forward human evolution to the next stage.

The new order will be a social-system guided by these selfless human beings, who are willing to sacrifice their life to bring progress and evolution of the human specie. Where to find them? How to structure the society where they may act as guides, and give shape to a new order? What will be the nature of the political organ in which they may function, and which they may shape? How will they interact with people, and represent the will of the people to achieve liberty and freedom of more meaningful kind, than what the market culture offers today? How will they be able to counteract the tendencies of human nature, which have colored the history of the human race so far? Will it be anything similar to what we know from history, or will it be a totally different world?

Purpose

Purpose of the change is to free mankind from the forces of history which have kept the human civilization a prisoner of power-loving individuals and groups, who have maintained their dominance since the formation of institutions of state and religion. It seeks to change the present order, which has emerged through an alliance of military and religious men with the businessmen and traders, who have risen during the colonial time, and are primarily driven by the interests of profits and individual gains at the expense of the misery of the majority of mankind. Instead of the lower-nature of man, still deciding the fate of humanity, as it has developed in the present consumer-culture of the monopoly-capitalist market-order, the enlightened-world wants to educate, inform and make human beings aware of the potentials of life, which exists beyond the animal instincts. It seeks to elevate human consciousness to a higher stage, and make use of the higher power of the mind in building an enlightened civilization, where man may realize his/her potential as the bearer of a cosmic-mind. It aspires to protect the freedom, liberty and possibility to enjoy the life of a "higher-man" by developing governing structure of the society, which will eliminate the advantages, which the traditional players of history have enjoyed until now. It also sees the necessity to free social-political development from the hands of the technocratic rule, which has developed in the recent time, in order to perpetuate an economic injustice, where the middle class consumers are being used as the means to achieve the goal of the rich and the powerful, while exploiting the poor, who supply labour and toil at the conditions dictated by the investors and their supporters in the power-elite. The purpose of the enlightened-order is to resist the abuse of technological innovation and communication, whose aim is to dehumanize human beings by turning them into animals living by consuming products, and creating distorted view of life as a bonanza of "happiness" to be enjoyed in a market place, without any vision, meaning and purpose. It wants to inspire mankind to respond to the call of the "higher-man" to fulfil the journey of life as an enlightened being, who bears the power of the cosmic-mind, and thus create a civilization where human beings may find meaning in life in love, compassion and sacrifice.

Goals

The goal is to build a foundation and structure of governance which will be able to give shape to the vision and realize the purpose under the guidance of the principles enshrined in the "Enlightened Manifesto of Civil and Political Rights" and "Enlightened Manifesto of Economic Social and Cultural Rights". It will focus on building Civic-organs at all levels of social organization whose mission will be to empower, educate and create awareness about the enlightened society keeping in mind the vision and purposes to be fulfilled. The activities of the people, through the mediation of these organs will bear the spirit of the enlightened society. The government will ensure open and free interactions in the Civil-organs at all levels of the society through discussions, dialogues and debates, and protect organs from abuse of personal interests of any power-loving individual, or group. The main mission of the Civic-organs will be to explain the contents of the Enlightened Manifesto of Civil and Political Rights and Economic, Social and Cultural Rights and generate discussions and debates in the society. By building infra-structures of modern communication, and helping to build networks among the Civil-organs at different levels, and within the same level, the government will commit itself to strengthen the pillars which may bear the structure of the "Enlightened-order". It will thus ensure the functioning of a law-bound society, which cannot be manipulated and corrupted by the remnants of power which still survives from the old-system as it exists in the present world-order.

List of Major Goals

Build Classless Society

Recognizing the superiority of the values on which the ideas of the enlightened world are based, over the ones which have prompted the development of an unjust world in the past, the new order sets as its goal to build a classless society where every individual may enjoy equal dignity and respect and the possibility to contribute in the progress of the social-political development.

Ensure Security of Life

The enlightened-order gives highest priority to the security of life against hunger and basic needs, and protection of liberty and freedom to develop one's potential as a human being possessing higher-level of consciousness beyond the needs of physical survival.

Bring Enlightened Democracy to Life

It will pursue the goal of meaningful participation of all without any discrimination of race, culture and gender where everybody is fully aware of the possibilities of development and the rights they are entitled to. In an enlightened democracy, where people are equipped with knowledge and information through the Civic-organs, social and political participations will be meant to secure complete transparencies and eliminate all forms of corruption from all spheres of life.

Establish Economic Justice

Its goal is to dismantle the institutional structure and mechanism which have grown out of the old feudal system and colonial history, and remove the oligarchs, who may aim at gaining control over resources in their hands in order to shape the developments of the economic life of the society to their advantage. The main goal of the economic justice will be to clean the society from the presently functioning "casino-culture" of wild financial speculations in a market driven by values, which intends to create money from "nothing". It will remove monopoly capitalism, supported by present banking system which dominates the world, and replace it with a just global system where people will possess the power to decide how economic transactions and benefits should be distributed and ensured. People`s representatives will manage the banks, and steer the development of the economic infrastructures, while the Civic-organs and the Government will guide and help them in pursuing the desired path of justice.

Foundation of a Universal Culture

The goal of the universal culture will be remove barriers among human beings due to class, caste and belief and bring an end to all forms of discrimination including race and gender. The new culture will set up support centres under the guidance of the Civic-organs to promote universal culture free from religious dogmatism and traditional practices driven by illiteracy and ignorance. It will seek to keep scientific knowledge at the helm of the new cultural order while creating openness to frontiers of experiences, which may not be understood by using the knowledge of science alone. While recognizing the spiritual nature of man, the enlightened culture will take distance from religious institutions, which may deprive the human beings of the benefits of scientific knowledge, and the freedom to explore the frontiers of life outside ignorance-bound narrow traditions of age-old culture. By recognizing the superiority of the universal culture over all other cultures, which may have hampered the development of the human beings towards a "higher-man", all institutions of religions, which may have played political roles in exploiting the human beings, should be dismantled, and replaced by cultural institutions promoting universal values. In this new cultural-order the Civic-organs will set the guidelines for public entertainment and culture, which will emphasizes on the nature of man as a creative being, who seeks to experience the greater realms of the mind beyond the instinctual pleasures and squandering of life in meaningless "fun".

Environmental Protection

The new order will keep guard against the destruction of nature, which supports human life participating together with millions of other species, in sustaining a fine-tuned ecosystem on Earth. All activities of development which may jeopardize the harmonious existence with nature will be avoided.

Build Peace And Contain Conflicts

Among other goals will be to demilitarize the world and work against the formation of military and economic alliances (reminiscent of the twentieth century) and free the international organizations from the hegemony of a few powerful nations with colonial history. Any intervention of one group of nation, enjoying military-technological and financial superiority over others and motivated by the desire to maintain hegemony over other nations, must be prohibited. Instead, it should be replaced by principles set by the highest Civic-Organ established in the global level, which may intervene on behalf of mankind, in situation when enlightened-order may face severe threats of its existence. The enlightened-order will also develop mechanisms to handle conflicts, which may arise among nations and religions (existing in the present cultural diversity) before a peaceful world may emerge from the present world-order, which verges on chaos today.

Foundation and Structure

The basic starting point of building this system will be the existence of a few enlightened human beings living in a community. These human beings will form a civil-committee, which will spear head the development and success of the system in a structure consisting of a small cluster of population- like, for example, a village. They will be the "enlightened" men/women of the village. These "enlightened" persons may come from any class, creed, gender and profession. They will be identified by their words and deeds, and their engagement in promoting the rights declared in the "Enlightened manifesto of Civil and Political Rights" and "Enlightened manifesto of Economic, Social and

Cultural Rights" (they are not the same as the UN Declarations, I shall come back to these manifestoes later). The main agenda of the civic-committee will be to teach, guide, explain and inform people in their community about the new order, so that people may participate in a meaningful way in constructing their own future, while they choose the governing organs through election. Instead of promoting party agendas, as is done in modern democracy today, they will promote the Universal agenda carrying new visions of mankind.

This civic-committee will replace the idea of the presently functioning party system. Their activities will include (beside those mentioned before) the project of engaging the people in the community in issues of common concern, keep vigilance over the violations which may occur, report violations to the governing organ accredited with the authority to project the population and form a network through which people as a whole may easily react and ask for remedy. Their task will be also to involve people in the social networking, which may generate cohesion, understanding and solidarity and create a climate of meaningful debate.

The head of the community will choose the members of the civic-committee, and be its head. Among others his/her task will be to see to the successful functionary of the organ in fulfilling the aimed objectives (I shall come back later to the question "who will choose the head?"). After the establishment of the Civil-organ, election to different committee taking care of the social-political, economic and cultural developments of the society will be held under the supervision of an election committee (later about who will choose election commissioner). Anyone in the civil committee may suggest any candidate: To qualify, the candidate must have served in the governance of the society or been a member of similar civil-organ. It may resemble Chinese direct election in the village level. However, it is very different: There is no party, who can dictate. Instead of party members of the civil committee, on whom people have trust and faith, will suggest candidates, who will abide by the "Enlightened manifestos", which protect freedom and rights of all in a meaningful way.

Structure

The people will directly choose members of the law-giving committee who will decide the principles and rules in building the social-order. These law-giving organs will chart out the goals of development, and the nature of freedom and liberty which the society should promote and advocate. They will become the guiding force of the society aspiring to establish the reign of the "higher-man". The law-giving committee, in turn, will appoint the members of the executive-committee, who will be entitled to implement the ideas and realize the goal of the enlightened society. The law-giving committee will also appoint the election committee, who will accept the qualification of the candidates, and arrange and supervise the election, and authorize the legality of the election result. Similarly, the law-giving organ will choose the members of the judicial organ, who will bear the responsibility of enforcing law equally to all, and protecting every individual citizen in enjoying security of a just society, which cannot be violated by any form of corruption.

The members of the Executive-committee and Judicial-committee will choose the head of the society, who will lead the Civic-committee and carry the authority to guide the media-culture, including the way people may be informed about the developments in the society. Under the advice of the Election committee, the law-giving body may remove the head and ask the Executive-committee and Judicial-committee to appoint a new person.

Among other functions of the head: He/she will be responsible in reporting the achievements of the Executive-committee and Judicial-committee and suggest new ideas and point out flaws. He/she will also choose representative to the structure which exists above the village level.

Thus the social-order will form an entangled network, where individual human activities and actions will be answerable to others, and guided by a common vision and goal which will serve all with equal effect.

Another new idea of this enlightened-order will be the presence of similar structures at different levels of population clustering. In the next-upper level, above the village, will lie the sub-district level (or a township). The governing structure will be very similar in this level to what may exist in the village level. The main difference will be that while in the village level, the election will be direct, in the higher-level it will be indirect election where the representatives from the village level will elect the members of the law-giving council, who in turn will choose the Executive-council, Judicial-council and the Election-council (committees in village level are called councils in the higher level).

The head in the higher-level will be responsible for networking among the civil-committees in the village level and ensuring free and trustworthy information flow across the villages. He/she will become responsible for the establishment of civic-council in the sub-district level. The civil-council in this level will consist of members represented by the Civil-Committees in the Village-level. The representation to the Civil-Council will be made by the individual Civil-Committees. The main activities of the Civil-council will be to give feedbacks to the village level and help them strengthen and consolidate their power in guiding the population. In the next level, i.e. the district level, the hierarchical repetition of similar order will continue. It will proceed to the level of provinces and state. May be, it can even embrace the entire World as an organization.

The existence of this order can be harmonious, only if the smaller units embedded in larger units get enough help and support from the larger structures, and at the same time, the smaller units provide outputs which the larger units need for its survival. I shall come back to these local and global relations later. At this moment I shall expand on the system operating at the village level.

Chapter 9
HOW ENLIGHTENED-ORDER MAY WORK?

To many the ideas of the enlightened world may appear out of tune with the reality of the world and what history tells us. The dynamics shaping the world appear very different from what the enlightened world envisages.

Though history and reality of the existing social order is a result of the interactions of different competing groups in the world and projections of human nature, it does not represent the higher man living in us all. It only accounts for the period of history when the instinct bound nature of us which has triumphed and made us captive of a social system from which we need to free ourselves.

The desire of man to overpower others, rob others of their opportunities and wealth, and impose one's hegemony creating insecurities and misery of life of people, who are weak, speak of the lowest level of human nature. At this level, human beings do not see life beyond their animal instincts which deprive them of the power to build a higher form of civilization. Success of capitalism is the story of this lower-man.

The scientific theories of the origin of the universe and evolution of life have also fuelled the development of the system where animal nature of man has gained the priority. Big-bang tells us that there is no meaning and purpose behind creation and all have started as an accident. In this accidental world life has begun as an equally accidental occurrence, when organic molecules have joined by a flick of accidents to form the macro-molecules of life. These macro-molecules, caught into the laws of nature, have gradually formed more complex life-forms, finally bringing the existence of human species on Earth. Here competitions for survival and development of life by preying on the others and building strategies of defence around one's own are seen as the right modes of conduct for an intelligent creature.

The way human history has developed during the modern time, speaks of this unethical and immoral nature of man, which is characteristic of human beings who have not discovered higher human possibilities through modes of co-operation and exchange, which may secure life of all. Life of the higher-man adopts a new mode, which teaches man to share, help and empower others in order to help them find ways to secure livelihood. It requires from man the ability to see life as an arena of love, brotherhood and compassion for all.

Many in the modern world may call this view of love and compassion as a sort of religious sentiment - a hangover from the past cultural teachings, which has no scientific basis. Science instead teaches man to compete, defeat and develop and accumulate wealth and power to create the ground of affluence and security for oneself which cannot be challenged and destroyed by others. Western nations have been doing this since the beginning of the modern time.

However, the emergence of the economic and military power of the Western countries was possible due to the scientific and technological innovations and creativity. The innovations of man, in turn,were utilized in accumulating wealth and power in a few hands. For the innovations to find a breeding ground one needed market and investment. The merchants and traders could provide this ground. However, their interests were nothing but profits and accumulation of wealth and power. Innovations were thus hijacked by the traders, and the bankers of that time. Then they gave shape to the modern culture. The creative man became the prisoners of the lower-nature. of the greedy. The modern civilization has progressed in the same path since then.

Not only the creative man, but also the spiritual-man has remained captive in the hands of the profit-making economic class exercising hegemony over political power. Traditional monarchs, as well as religious clergies have succumbed to their interests. The churches in the West had sided with the capitalists in order to find their own breeding ground outside the boundaries of their own countries. Similarly, monarchs had risen and fallen, as consequences of economic power game under the control of the bankers and the merchant class. The same appears to be true today.

Challenges of an Enlightened World

The challenges of the enlightened world are to understand the mechanisms by which human history and civilization have become prey to the lower-nature of man. By recognizing the necessity of evolution of man towards a higher-path, one needs to prescribe ways and means to free the higher nature of man from the captivity of the profit-loving human beings. In this regard one must be guided by a vision and a view of the unity of living world and the harmony and the order which may bring freedom of the higher-man. One needs to understand the links that exist among institutions which perpetuate the dominance and hegemony of the financial class and their collaborators coming from other cultural areas. The understanding of their relations to the military-industrial complex is most essential to find ways to free humanity from the evil forces of our time.

Main point is: One must not accept the reality of history, as it is today, as the foundation of building the future of mankind. It should be considered as erroneous and fallen path where humanity has been led by traders and bankers of the 18th and 19th century Europe. Recognizing it as a path of the lower-man, human beings should throw away the existing system and replace it with an ethical and moral[2] system that may bring human evolution to a higher-path. We need a system

2 See "Book of Will and World- A Foundation of Moral Universalism" by Anup Rej, Books of Existence, 2014.

change - a radical overthrow of the monopoly-capitalism in the first place (instead of making economic theories by keeping capitalism as something sacrosanct).

One argues that only profits and personal freedom to make gains and accumulate power motivate most human being to be innovative, creative and keep themselves engaged in economic activities that can bring new innovations and rapid development.

This is the position of those, who believe that there is no gain in making sacrifices for others, and working for the cause of mankind at the expense of one's own personal interests. It is the belief of those, who do not see the way everything are dependent and entangled with each other, and do not know that the source of one's own happiness and peace is the happy and peaceful life of the other's. They do not understand that the true source of lasting freedom for oneself is the freedom of the fellow human beings, which can only be created with the power of love and being compassionate to the sufferings of others.

Those, who reject compassion and love as a sentimental religious attitude, in order to hold on to their animal behaviour, seem to be dominating the cultural premise of the technological age today. The progress and success of this lower nature of the mind must be challenged by the enlightened women and men who are willing to build the new premise for a higher civilization.

As long as the elements, which threaten the realization of an enlightened democracy all over the world, are not brought under the control of a universal body, which will have the authority to deal justice in furthering premises of freedom for mankind, the idea of peace will remain elusive. In a world, where different nations conceive democracy and freedom in different ways, and practice and implement them in the context of their individual culture following narrow political interest, leaving the issue of human progress to an organization like the UN, as it is now, where every nation is trying to find opportunities for their interests, will not help to create any enlightened world.

Where and When Enlightened Democracy May Work?

The ideas of the enlightened democracy cannot be implemented in a society unless the citizens are free from hunger and basic needs and are exposed to knowledge and information with which they may explore the conditions of freedom available in life. It requires a society that may provide access to high level of education and awareness of the possibilities that may lie outside the beliefs and ideologies which form the backbones of the existing social structures. Only in a society where human beings feel secure in exploring the possibilities of one`s development without being threatened by authorities jeopardizing the search of freedom and meaning of life, the enlightened democracy can take roots. It is a society of enlightened human beings, who understand the possibilities of life as an evolving being and willing to explore into higher and higher realms of consciousness, which can only be achieved through joint efforts. In such a society, people are stimulated to analyse conditions of life with reason without bearing prejudices, and encouraged to make independent judgment about the developments of the society with the aim of correcting its course. People are given opportunities so that all may contribute with ideas and actions in shaping the evolution. Using knowledge as the foundation of an enlightened life, when people are inspired to engage in creative activities with the aim of changing the social reality, which may open greater dimensions of freedom, the spirit of the enlightened society may come forth. By creating conditions of free choice and thus building a foundation of a new reality, not dictated mechanically by the forces of nature, or coerced by existing structures of power governing the social and political dynamics, the enlightened society offers ways to recreate the world according to higher needs of the mind.

However, it does not profess a random development in different directions following different ideas. It adheres to the vision of development which may unite all to build a social environment of harmony where all may live in peace. It connects man to its cosmic nature, where all are entangled in a whole fulfilling the meaning of a purposeful design (cosmos is not an accidental random manifestation of laws as big-bang theory teaches, but a purposeful creation arising from a cosmic mind where existence of the tinniest micro bodies to the largest cosmic structures are all manifestations of a cosmic consciousness). To create such a world one would need an education system and an enlightened civil society that will provide guidance to people. Knowledge and power of creativity alone are not sufficient to attain the awareness and goal directed towards the higher evolution of man. People will need guides in exploring the possibilities of freedom and understanding how to work in fulfilling the vision of an enlightened world. Thus the enlightened world envisions the rise of the enlightened teachers and guides. It will be a society free of fundamentalism of religion, belief or ideology and open to all ideas which may bring progress with universal appeal to all, who seek a common frontier of development for mankind without consideration of race, culture or nation.

Civic-Organ

The existence of the Civic-Organ is the most central element in the Enlightened World-order. It will be the basic foundations of all societies at all levels guiding people to find meaningful ways of choosing their own development. It will replace the religious societies who may operate in the public sphere, and be the act as the meeting place for ideological differences among contending views about economic, political and cultural matters. It will be the voice of the universal man, seeking an enlightened path of human evolution. It will inspire every human being to learn the universal language of freedom, liberty and justice, and help them to know how to avoid the drag towards the lower nature bound to instincts similar to what exists in the animal kingdom. It will be the voice of love and compassion for all, and a way forward to know one's own higher nature.

Civic-organs will act as the centres for raising public awareness about one's greater possibilities, and transmit knowledge and information which may strengthen brotherhood of man of all races, cultures and help to open doors to explore new frontiers of creativity through co-operation, discussion and debate.

Civic-Organ Will Be Endowed With the Following Tasks

Promote the knowledge of the cosmos and the nature of human life and its interdependence with the living and nonliving world which forms the surrounding environment (this will act as the foundation of the ideas of an Enlightened World).

Teach human beings about the relationship that exist between the micro and macro-cosmos, and help them to see themselves as the bearer of a "cosmic mind".

Teach about what is moral and ethical in the perspective of what exists in nature, and how the things in the cosmos are ordered and organized.

Teach about what is the higher-nature of man, and who is an enlightened person and how to attain that enlightened stage?

Inspire human beings to seek the power lying within himself/herself to bring changes in history.

Explain the way the social and political evolution has occurred in history and how different forces have shaped the social-order we see today.

Teach that human security does not lie in competition and winning over others, but in co-operation, understanding of other's needs, and sharing with others, one's own point of advantage. The security for all is the best security for any individual, which can only be gained through collaboration. By defeating others one may win wealth and properties, but at the same time may loose the security which one may enjoy in the spirit of sharing with others and showing respect for others' life.

Teach that the human beings are not animals of consumption: Consumption culture gives man only the freedom to live a meaningless life driven by primitive instincts.

Explain the way the ideas of religion have evolved and the religious institutions have taken shapes, supported by political powers, seeking dominance and wealth.

Explain the true essence of a "Spiritual" man.

Open the doors to understand the relations between "religion" and science.

Make aware of our intimate relations with the environment and help us to be responsible actors in relations to nature so that our own existence, and the existence of other species on Earth may not be jeopardized.

Inform all citizens about the manifestos of the enlightened society, which will guide the law-giving organs of the society in formulating rules and policies which govern the society (the manifestos will include the Civil and Political Rights, as well as the Economic, Social and Cultural Rights).

Create openness to the universal values and ideas and the necessity to make further progress in comprehending the fuller possibilities of human life, which may not yet be enshrined in the manifestos.

Teach and debate about what is economic justice, and make assessment of the rules and principles which may create the foundation of justice in the society.

Teach the value of sharing one's ingenuity and innovation with others in order to improve the quality of life of the community as a whole (instead of using the innovations in the pursuit of exploiting the others).

Provide the people with the knowledge of modern communication which may make the society more cohesive and strong, and inspire people in building social networking, which may make human beings more responsive to the desire for meaning of life only attainable by sharing ideas and thoughts helpful to other human beings.

Create forums, involving audio-visual interactions across geographical and cultural barriers, where anyone in the community may freely join discussion and debate.

Steps to Build Enlightened Society

Beside the Civic-Organ, which lies at the apex of the enlightened-order led by people, who would teach and inform the population about the ideas of the new-system, another central pillar of such a society will be the educational system which should inject necessary knowledge and awareness in order to help younger generation to create the enlightened-order. By creating, already at an early stage of education and social upbringing, an openness and respect for all life, and informing about the higher nature of human freedom and richer possibilities of life as a human being aware of their greater capacity of the mind, one may build the steps to create the envisioned world.

The enlightened education should stimulate different aspects of human mind by inspiring man to pursue Path of Knowledge, Path of Creativity, Path of Contemplation and Path of Compassion and Love. The main doctrine will be to build a foundation of values based on knowledge and awareness of the unity and wholeness that exists in a purposeful existence of the nature. These values will help mankind to bring peace, harmony and justice in the world.

Is it only dream?

Of course, it is a dream: The ideas presented here may seem to bear much reality with the way the society in modern time operates, and the elements on which the dynamics of the present world-order is based. To some it may appear as fa dream out of tune with the forces of the modern time.

However, one should remember that without such dreams the human

HOW ONE MAY START BUILDING THE FOUNDATION OF THE ENLIGHTENED WORLD?

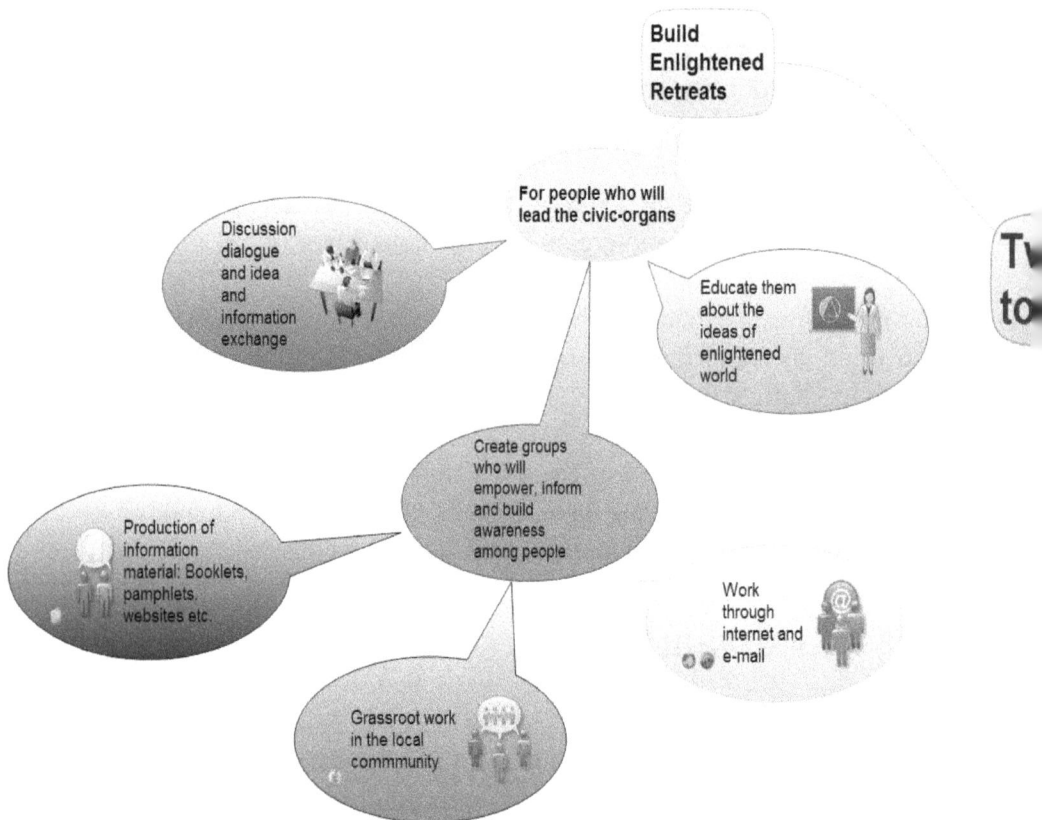

Build Enlightened Retreats

For people who will lead the civic-organs

Discussion dialogue and idea and information exchange

Educate them about the ideas of enlightened world

T
to

Create groups who will empower, inform and build awareness among people

Production of information material: Booklets, pamphlets, websites etc.

Work through internet and e-mail

Grassroot work in the local commmunity

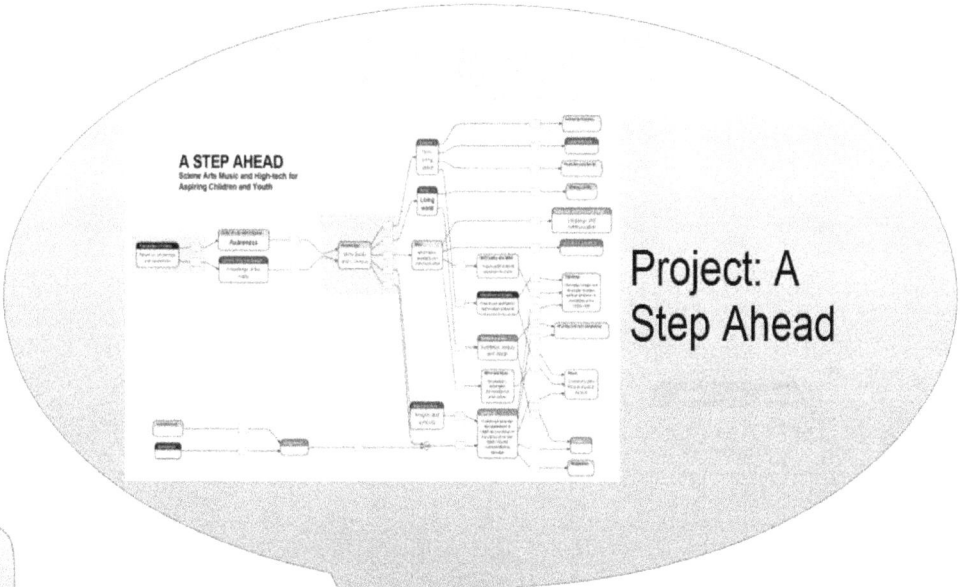

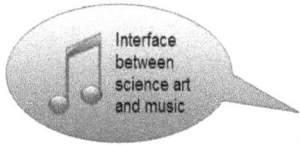

A STEP AHEAD

Sciene Arts Music and High-tech for
Aspiring Children and Youth

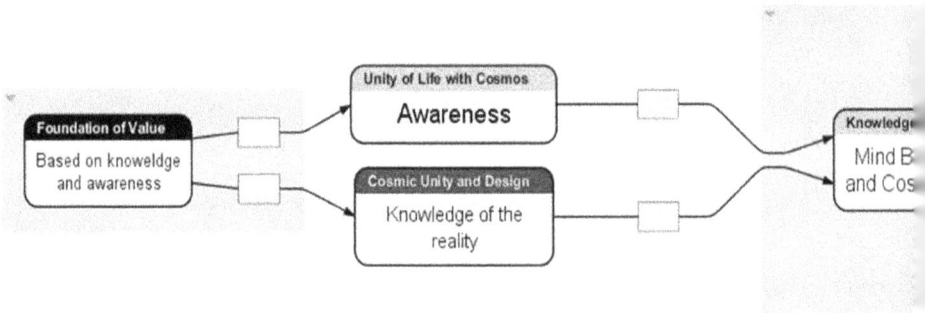

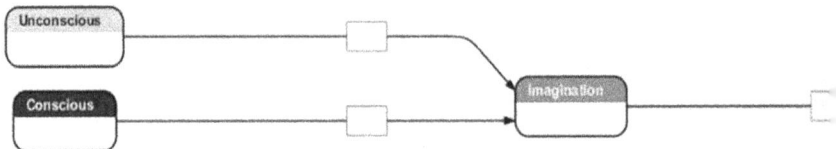

Foundation of Value

Based on knoweldge
and awareness

Unity of Life with Cosmos

Awareness

Cosmic Unity and Design

Knowledge of the
reality

Knowledge

Mind B
and Cos

Unconscious

Conscious

Imagination

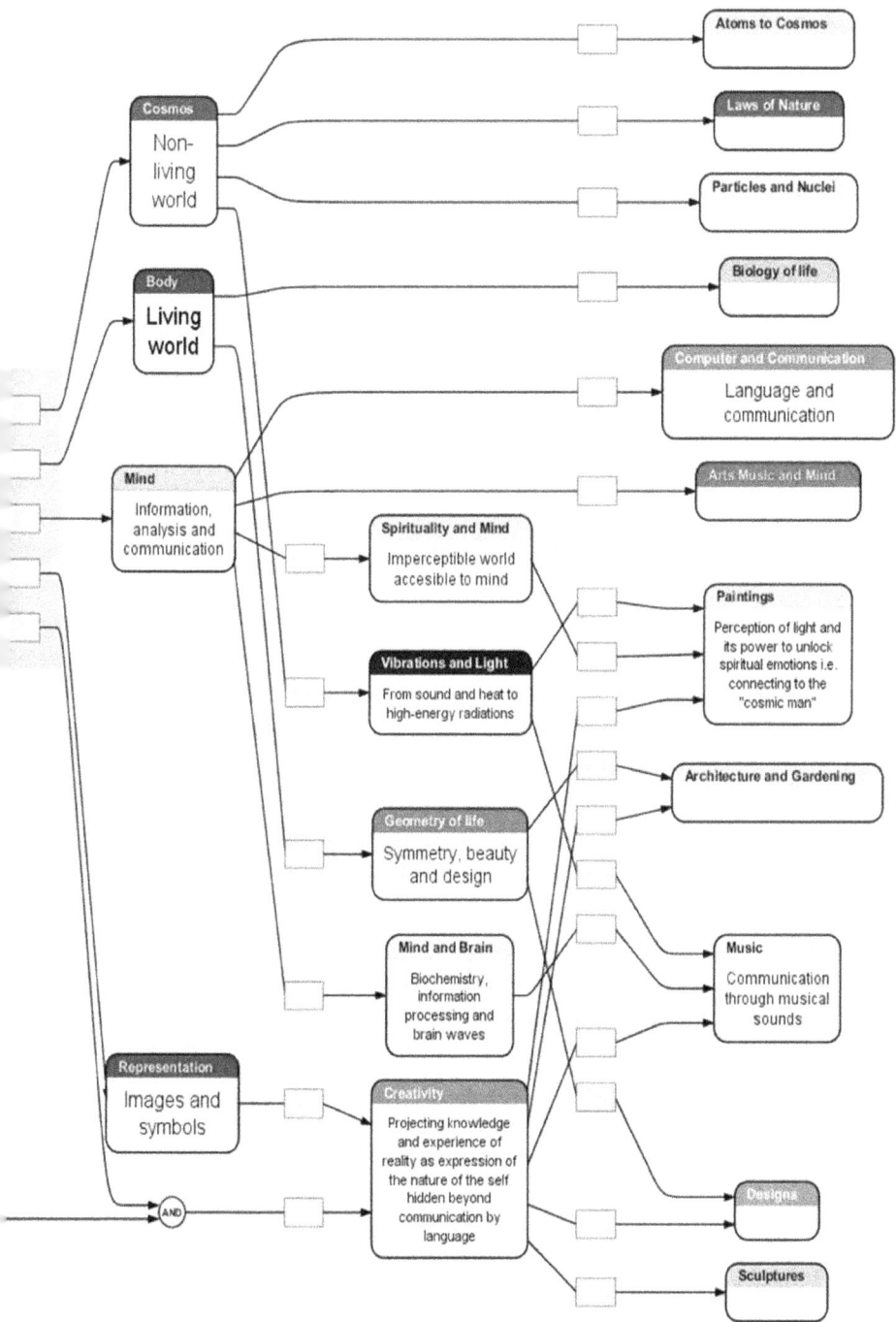

Cosmos
Non-living world

- Atoms to Cosmos
- Laws of Nature
- Particles and Nuclei

Body
Living world

- Biology of life

Mind
Information, analysis and communication

- **Computer and Communication**
  Language and communication
- **Arts Music and Mind**

Spirituality and Mind
Imperceptible world accesible to mind

Vibrations and Light
From sound and heat to high-energy radiations

Geometry of life
Symmetry, beauty and design

Mind and Brain
Biochemistry, information processing and brain waves

Representation
Images and symbols

Creativity
Projecting knowledge and experience of reality as expression of the nature of the self hidden beyond communication by language

Paintings
Perception of light and its power to unlock spiritual emotions i.e. connecting to the "cosmic man"

Architecture and Gardening

Music
Communication through musical sounds

Designs

Sculptures

AND

civilization cannot make progress. If human beings accept the confinements of the conditions which define the characteristics of the society at
a particular time and do not aspire to create a new world, the evolution
would stagnate. Who could have ever believed only 20 years ago about
the way human beings now communicate by using e-mail, 3G-4G mobile phones and access information by using internet? Who could have
ever imagined only a few years ago that the entertainment industry of
videos, music and libraries of books will soon be accessible from any
part of the world at every place on Earth for downloading from the
"air" (wireless)? If one talked about such an idea only a generation ago,
it would have been regarded as a dream. May be, such dreams are the
foundation of human progress. They provide the sources of power of
creativity with which one may change the environment,and decondi-
tion the factors which define the nature of the so-called "reality", which
seems close and inevitable once those conditions have taken hold of
life.

"Reality", which we perceive so closely, is not any God-given circumstance, or heavenly prescription destined for ever. The human beings themselves are authors of such "reality" which involves actions
and processes of engagement which can be changed and modified
through mental-pursuits. The physical reality sometimes may appear
unchangeable and fixed, which sets barriers and brings challenges on
the way of the survival of species. At the same time they may provide
opportunities to find new directions of evolution, depending on how
human beings are capable of reorienting themselves in different ways.
It means that the reality does not conduct the forces of life - instead,
the dreaming and imaginative human beings can shape the "reality" by
the way they engage themselves in the so-called reality. It is the power
of the will, and the capacity of imagination, supported by the knowledge available to human beings, which form the essence of the "reality"
that we ourselves may create.

When we tune in to TV channels, or open the pages of news media and
watch the "News of the World", or "Business News", the "reality" projected through the CRT, LCD, or LED screens, impinge on our mind,
as if everything we watch, listen, or read carry unchangeable and inef-

fable forces of time. The conditions of the moment of history appear as certain, inevitable and real affecting what we do and how we live. Any ideas contradicting this immediate condition may seem as dream and imagination.

Once the "reality" is reshaped by using the power of imagination and capacity of the mind to reorient and recondition the premises of the "reality", it re-emerges in a new way while replacing the perception of "reality" with a new perspective. The "reality" thus takes shape according to the way we dream and engage in changing the circumstances in which we live.

The reality of history, which has emerged as the present economic and political system, is similarly a product of human ideas and endeavours. They can be changed by adopting a new way of orienting ourselves in the circumstances of life, which define the reality of history through which the human civilization is passing now.

Since the beginning of the modern civilization, the history has taken shape according to interests and ideas of particular groups of people, whose main purpose were to dominate, exploit and accumulate wealth and power in a few hands. However, it has not gone uncontested. The ideologies, challenging this individual greed while dreaming to bring a social-political change, which would serve the interests of a greater part of humanity, has risen during the twentieth century. However, these new ideologies have failed to implement the humanitarian ideas because the people involved in realizing the ideas have succumbed to the temptation of greed and power corruption.

To many, the individual greed and power corruption appear to be the inevitable reality of history behind any social-political dynamics. When one watches the way the stock-market speculators, and banking experts control the dynamics of history of modern time, or the way different governments react to the flow of capital or scarcity of investments affecting the economic life, it leaves no illusion that reality of today's history can not be changed by a few dreaming individuals. Those who fall outside the power structure act as pawns in a social-economic process manipulated by the people controlling the economic and political institutions.

One may argue that what is happening in history reflects the true nature of man, and these people are representative of the winning forces in the society. The one, who is more clever and mightier, is destined to come out as successful actors in history.

The vision of the enlightened world takes distance from this view. It rejects the idea that the human beings are nothing but economic animals and do not share the understanding that the success of mankind lies in economic and political competitions for wealth and power. Though the foundation of history, in which we live today, is prepared by women and men, who may subscribe to the idea of the supremacy of the more intelligent and powerful, the vision of the enlightened world considers such views as hindrance for the fulfilment of greater human potentials. The human beings prescribing such view are deprived of the understanding of the higher nature of life. By building a social-political order, which serve the lower-nature bound to instincts, they have created a civilization which has led us to a darkened realm of the mind. This darkened-path has now become the inevitable "reality" of history of the modern man.

Only by using the higher-power of the mind, one may bring mankind away from this development of history. Without being dazzled by the economic theories of the academicians, who serve the present system, or being overwhelmed by the "wisdom" of the bankers and the market experts, who feed on and grow in strength by exploiting the system, we need to wake up and "dream" about a new future for mankind.

Unless we "dream and are able to restate the goal and meaning of human civilization in a new way based on higher-nature of our mind, the evolution of human life will remain conditioned by the animal instincts as it has done for centuries. We need to rise above this primitive understanding of ourselves and conceive human beings instead as bearers of the cosmic-mind.

This book is a call for "dreaming" about a new-world and a guide for those who wish to understand the forces which has created the "reality" of history, where we find ourselves. Its purpose is to inspire the new generation to think about how we may act and change the conditions of our life by the power of "dream" that bears the forces derived from our higher cosmic nature.

This is a call for an "awakened dream", where the mind may remain awakened by the greater vision of us and the cosmos. The ideas of this book derive inspiration from the knowledge of science, and the experiences of mankind that surpasses the realm of science. It is a dream of the "awakened man", a "vision of the enlightened being", who sees oneself as one with the living and the nonliving world.

It is a call to step into a new universe outside and within ourselves and invitation to create a new reality of history following the rhythms of the universe which vibrate in unison within our cell as well as in the stars.

Epilogue

The enlightened democracy described in this book floats mostly in a lofty sphere of ideas. How one may implant these ideas in the social-political reality of the world today will constitute the subject matter of a new book by the author.

About the author

Anup Rej was born in Kolkata, India in a liberal Bengali family where the spirit of the nineteenth and early twentieth century Bengali renaissance still remained alive through a passionate engagement in Eastern and Western literature, arts, philosophies and social-political ideologies. From early childhood he imbibed ideas of universal values and love for knowledge. He received his Ph.D. in theoretical Nuclear Physics from the University of Calcutta before he moved to Oslo, Norway in 1971. After working in the University of Oslo and University of Trondheim in theoretical Nuclear Physics and Elementary Particle Physics, he went to live in Switzerland with his Norwegian wife – a career diplomat - whom he married in 1975. Later, while his wife was serving as a diplomat in the Norwegian Permanent Mission at the UN in New York on issues of human rights and humanitarian affairs, he developed deep interests in the situations of human rights and conflicts in the world.

While in Switzerland (Bern and Geneva) his activities in physics shifted towards cosmology, which was fashionable among the particle physicist at CERN during the early 1980s. His interests in a new theory of the universe began at that time. However, his career as a physicist came abruptly to an end with the death of their only son Ånun, who was bereaved of life only at the age of ten in a gondola accident on the

Alps in 1990. He left physics and went in an inner journey in search of meaning and purpose of life. During this period he wrote an epic called "Tathagata -A Divine Comedy for Our Time" relating the wandering of the universal man (of whom all individuals are parts), who comes and goes life after life. In this book of poetry, music, philosophy, mythology and religion he summarized his understanding of the nature of human consciousness, and the meaning of existence.

He returned to physics once again when he moved to Seoul in 1994, where his wife served as the Ambassador of Norway to the Republic of Korea. At that time his interest switched to chaos theory and non-inear dynamics. With it, he first proposed the multi-fractal nature of a designed universe in 1999 in a lecture at the University of Oslo. Since then he has been pursuing the ideas of the creation of a universe without beginning and end, where time exists in the background of a timeless design (Timelessness in Time).

During his stay in Seoul, he made a debut as an artist with an exhibition of oil paintings entitled, "Art Without Beginning and End: Moving Through the Cycle of Life, Death and Resurrection" at Seoul Arts Centre. Since then his activities in arts, science, literature and philosophy etc. have all converged towards exploring the cosmic nature of human existence, which is inseparably entangled with the micro and macro cosmos.

During the period 2000-2005 he has lived in Bangkok as a spouse of an Ambassador, while developing his ideas about new cosmology and creating multimedia-presentations of his different works for the digital age. At present he lives in Dhaka, where his wife serves as the Ambassador of Norway to Bangladesh. Parts of the book "Vision of an Enlightened World: Cosmic Perspective in Building a New Social-Political-Order" was written in Dhaka.

The links to his works on cosmology, art, literature, philosophy etc. can be found in the website: *http://MyJourney.EnlightenedWorld.net*

www.ingramcontent.com/pod-product-compliance
Lightning Source LLC
Chambersburg PA
CBHW020813300326
41914CB00075B/1740/J